MW00422722

LESSONS

FROM

LEADERS

VOLUME 1

LESSONS

FROM

LEADERS

VOLUME 1

PRACTICAL LESSONS
FOR A LIFETIME OF LEADERSHIP

Marshall Goldsmith, PhD
Sam K. Shriver, EdD
Kathy McDermott

Foreword by **Sandy Ogg**

LESSONS FROM LEADERS VOLUME 1 is published by,

LEADERSHIP STUDIES, INC. dba The Center For Leadership Studies.
280 Towerview Court
Cary, NC 27513
(919) 335-8763
situational.com

Printed in the United States of America
Leadership Studies, Inc. © 2020

For additional information or permissions to reproduce selections from this book,
please contact info@lessonsfromleadersbook.com.

FIRST EDITION

10 9 8 7 6 5 4 3 2 1

ISBN: 978-0-931619-13-7

For more information, visit lessonsfromleadersbook.com.

To Suzie Bishop

This book was your idea … and no one did more to put that vision into action than you! Sincere thanks for your leadership, stewardship, and friendship from start to finish!

Marshall, Sam & Kathy

CONTENTS

Each chapter starts with an author introduction that sets the stage for each leader's story.

FOREWORD

Disruptive change. Daunting risks. Increasing complexity. Rampant uncertainty.

The world today demands that we care about leadership, for leadership is the key to accomplishing together what we cannot accomplish as individuals.

When I worked for The Center for Leadership Studies back in the 1980s, Situational Leadership® was just beginning to hit its stride. I remember regular, deep discussions with the likes of Dr. Paul Hersey, Marshall Goldsmith, and Sam Shriver. We'd talk about leadership styles, behaviors, and competencies, literally trying out and playing with the foundational ideas of Situational Leadership® together. As the years went by and we went out into the world, we wove what we had learned together into our individual lines of work.

Since then, I've come to appreciate two things about leadership and learning even more. People learn the fundamental principles of leadership from other great leaders. And they master how to be a leader by applying those principles in diverse, real-world situations.

Nowadays, leaders are called on to do many things all at once. Create an inspiring vision of the future based on the "right" set of values. Lean into the many changes that vision will require. Enroll stakeholder groups throughout the ecosystem of their business in realizing that vision. Step onto the playing field with their talented teams and allies as everyone executes the critical plays that will make that future real. And all of this in situations marked by ~~disruptive change, daunting risks, increasing complexity, and rampant uncertainty.~~

The following compilation of insights, gathered from an array of leaders playing different roles across society over the past few years, points to some of the ageless principles leaders everywhere need to stay in touch with during these truly challenging times. I confess that, even before Sam asked me to have a look at this manuscript, I already admired everything about Frances Hesselbein, Alan Mulally, and Jim Yong Kim: They are people I know personally whose leadership has had an extraordinary impact in the world. By the time I had finished reading about the other exemplary individuals in *Lessons from Leaders*, I had decided to make it my mission to get to know all of them and their work much better.

If you are a leader who is up to something big in this world, you would be wise to, at the very least, disrupt yourself by taking on some of their ideas.

Sandy Ogg
Founder, CEO.works

CONTRIBUTORS

Below is a list of the contributors who offered their personal and practical lessons on leadership:

David Brennan—CEO and executive director of AstraZeneca PLC from 2006-12 who spearheaded the transformation of the pharmaceutical giant into the realm of biologics.

Daryl Davis—award-winning musician who became a civil rights activist and best-selling author; credited with personally transforming the thinking of over 200 card-carrying Ku Klux Klan (KKK) members.

Madeleine Dean—the first of four women elected to Congress in 2018 from Pennsylvania; has a track record of passion on issues like addiction prevention, equal rights, and gun violence.

Jim Duncan—one of the Top Ten Sales Professionals in America, as identified by *Fortune Magazine*; helped grow computer leasing giant Comdisco from $60 million in annual revenue to over $4 billion.

Clarissa Etter-Smith—a courageous senior leader in a variety of Fortune 50 organizations. She advances people and causes and can always be counted on to say and, much more importantly, do "the right thing."

Ann Herrmann-Nehdi—chairwoman of Herrmann, a technology company that helps individuals and organizations worldwide understand their thinking to unleash hidden cognitive potential.

Frances Hesselbein—former Girl Scouts of the USA CEO, Presidential Medal of Freedom recipient with twenty-two honorary doctoral degrees, editor of the *Leader to Leader* journal, and chairman of the Hesselbein Forum at the University of Pittsburgh.

Jim Yong Kim—Korean American physician and anthropologist who was the twelfth president of the World Bank, seventeenth president of Dartmouth College, and the co-founder of Partners in Health.

Justin Morgan—progressive pastor of an innovative and rapidly growing church who is leading positive change in a historically traditional space.

Alan Mulally—aeronautical engineer who became an executive vice president of The Boeing Company, CEO of Boeing Commercial Airplanes, and president of Boeing Information, Space, and Defense Systems before becoming the CEO of the Ford Motor Company, where he orchestrated one of the most prolific turnarounds in corporate history.

Sheila Simon—professor of law and the former trailblazing lieutenant governor of Illinois who is the daughter of former U.S. Senator Paul Simon and State Representative Jeanne Hurley Simon.

Nancy Singer—global leadership development executive for an elite Fortune 50 company for much of her career; considered a true pioneer and champion for women in leadership.

Patrick Stokes—high school history teacher and football coach who figured out what he wanted to do with his life as a teenager and has gone on to shape the lives of kids ever since.

Pat Summitt—Hall of Fame women's basketball coach who won eight national championships, an Olympic gold medal, the Presidential Medal of Freedom, and The Arthur Ashe Courage Award.

Brett Williams—retired U.S. Air Force major general, director of operations U.S. Cyber Command, F-15 fighter pilot, co-founder and COO of IronNet cybersecurity, established keynote speaker and coach.

ACKNOWLEDGEMENTS

A special thanks, as always, to:

- our team at The Center for Leadership Studies for your dedication and passion for developing leaders

- Sarah McArthur for her sincerity, guidance, and support; and

- Michelle Eggleston Schwartz for her innate literary talent and being an absolute pleasure to work with

INTRODUCTION

There are some books by their very nature that need to be read cover to cover. Skipping around would make you crazy because the culminating narrative found in Chapter 6 would have little meaning without the background provided in Chapter 2 or the cascading plot detailed in Chapters 3-5. With that in mind please know this:

> This book *can* be consumed from front to back, but it certainly doesn't have to be!

As a matter of fact, our advice would be to scan the table of contents and become familiar with the leaders that have shared their stories, then proceed in whatever sequence makes sense to you! Simply stated, and as we all know by now, leadership is different things to different people. What fully resonates with some of us might be irrelevant to others. If nothing else, this book is evidence of that assertion!

The other thing we know is that leadership happens "all over the place." By that we mean it is a multidirectional dynamic. It flows down (from boss to employee), laterally (from peer to peer), and up (from the base of your organization) in every imaginable setting (i.e., large and small companies, for-profit and nonprofit, public and private, etc.). The one thing every chapter in this book has in common is that it tells a story about a leader—someone who has taken the process of effectively influencing others seriously during their careers and has learned lessons along the way that have the potential to be instructive for us all.

There are several leaders you will probably recognize. Their accomplishments have been well chronicled in the public domain. There are other leaders that could best be described as having made their mark "in the trenches." They have distinguished themselves as leaders in settings that may not have attracted bright lights but were no less impressive. We have witnessed this reality repeatedly as our world has responded to COVID-19. Disruptive change provides leadership opportunities indiscriminately to those with or without the formal authority of elevated positions. We believe that assertion will be confirmed many times over by the pages that follow.

The spectrum of featured leaders includes:

Civil Rights Leader

- a civil rights activist who has a documented history of changing the hearts, minds, and behaviors of card-carrying disciples of hate and bigotry

Military Leader

- a retired Air Force general who spent most of his career as a fighter pilot before being put in charge as director of operations at U.S. Cyber Command

Religious Leader

- a pastor with a track record of leveraging doctrine to unite people with differing orientations of life, love, and the pursuit of happiness

Corporate Leaders

- an executive director who could be counted upon to tell top management what everybody was convinced they were afraid to hear
- a sales executive who was a driving force in the transformation of a $60 million company into a global, multibillion-dollar industry leader

Coaches

- a legendary, Hall of Fame women's basketball coach who transcended her sport, won the Presidential Medal of Freedom, and left a legacy of true excellence
- a high school history teacher and football coach who has provided direction, motivation, perspective, and vision to thousands of kids

Political Leaders

- a principled politician with a calling to serve others who became the first woman from her state to be elected to the United States Congress
- a woman who was born into a prominent political family and went on to hold a prestigious office herself and change the face of politics in her state

Learning and Development Leaders

- a globally recognized, second-generation CEO of a company that teaches leaders how to effectively harness the unlimited potential that resides in their brains
- a successful line manager and director for a global company that became an accomplished steward of leadership and, in particular, of women in leadership

C-Suite Executives

Four top executives who, as individuals:
- engineered one of the most prolific turnarounds in corporate history
- became a trailblazing example for future generations of women leaders
- worked directly with President Obama to enact health-care reform
- made tangible progress in the ongoing fight against world hunger

It is our sincere hope that at least one of these stories will provide you with a blueprint of actionable advice, inspiration to fulfill your leadership potential, or perhaps ... both!

FRANCES HESSELBEIN

Author Introduction

What image comes to mind for you when you consider "standing in the presence of greatness?" By chance, would it include staring down into the eyes of a five-foot-tall, well beyond typical retirement-age woman? Candidly, it wasn't for us either until, of course, we had the opportunity to come face-to-face with Frances Hesselbein.

The first thing that hits you is "the eyes!" More accurately: It's the eyes, in combination with a wry smile, undoubtedly perfected throughout the years, that unmistakably communicates:

> "… this is going to be fun! I am so very glad we are together today … and I am genuinely interested in you … and I am interested in the things that are of interest to you."

All of this and more is communicated nonverbally in the seconds that transpire before a word is ever spoken. Immediately, and somewhat unexplainably, you feel safe. You don't have to worry about playing a role or projecting a sense of competence or confidence. All you have to do is be the most real and transparent version of yourself.

This comes in handy because, as you start to look around her Park Avenue office, you notice there isn't one inch of wall space, desktop, or bookcase that doesn't have a personalized photograph of this diminutive "power broker" with a real-world leader. Some of these photos are recent and some are decades old. Some are with people you don't recognize, but many are with people you most certainly do: presidents, ambassadors, admirals, generals, famous CEOs, civic leaders, and more—the kinds of people you are used to seeing on the covers of magazines or with microphones shoved in their faces during crowded press conferences of one type or another. And all of a sudden it hits you. All of these people, at one time or another, were in a room with this kind and powerful lady. They saw the eyes! They saw the smile! They experienced the safety net and they also recognized they were, indeed, in the presence of greatness!

The on-camera interview begins and quickly becomes an hour of your life you know right away you will never forget. You learn things about history that catch you by surprise, for instance, that Hesselbein is a direct decedent of President John Adams who was the only person to sign the Declaration of Independence that had never owned a slave. Somehow, this doesn't surprise you in the least. On the heels of that candid insight, you receive one of the most practical reviews of diversity and inclusion imaginable (how simple it really is … and how difficult we go out of our way to make it). You hear a perspective on millennials that is fresh, invigorating, and delivered with the predictive conviction that only an experienced generational expert can provide. You hear a story about a grandmother in western Pennsylvania (almost a century ago) and her relationship with a gentleman, her laundryman, by the name of Mr. Yee. You are convinced (beyond reproach) everyone on the planet should hear this story at least once and examine their own lives through the lens of its wisdom.

As we believe the pages that follow will wholeheartedly attest, Hesselbein has forgotten more about leadership than the rest of us may ever know. Please enjoy!

"Leadership is a matter of how to be— not how to do."

- Frances Hesselbein

MISSION-FOCUSED

Frances Hesselbein

Lead from Within

In a few concise words, a mission statement clearly communicates the purpose, values, and goals of an organization. These carefully selected words connect people to the heart of the business and, ultimately, convey why they do what they do. These words embody the passion, dedication, and inspiration behind the company.

Just as a business operates with purpose, leaders must also maintain a core value system and live with intention. "When you think about it, we spend most of our lives learning 'how to do' and teaching other people 'how to do.' Yet, in the end, it is the quality and character of a leader that determines the results." Quite simply, "Leadership is a matter of how to be—not how to do," according to leadership advocate Frances Hesselbein.

Leadership comes from within and is core to who we are as individuals. Leadership is not a function of position; it is exemplified in our character and daily interactions with others. Being an effective leader cannot be obtained through a promotion or designation; the most ordinary person can be a leader. It starts with us.

Respect for All People

When she was eight years old, Hesselbein learned a valuable lesson about character and respect from her beloved grandmother. Her grandmother had seven children with her grandfather, who served as justice of the peace for over fifty years. In their home, they had a pipe organ with a shelf above the keyboard that held two beautiful, tall, ancient Chinese vases.

Every week Hesselbein would visit her grandmother and pleaded to play with the vases. And every week her grandmother would tell her no. One Saturday, when Hesselbein was feeling rather sure of herself, she stomped her feet at her grandmother and demanded in her worst tone that she be able to play with the vases. Instead of scolding Hesselbein for her behavior, her grandmother calmly led her over to a dark-red-velvet Victorian love seat facing the pipe organ and they sat down. Putting her arm around her shoulder, her grandmother shared the story behind the significance of the vases.

Long ago, when Hesselbein's mother was only eight years old, there was a Chinese laundryman, Mr. Yee, who came to the house every Tuesday to pick up her grandfather's shirts. And every Thursday he brought them back beautifully washed, starched, and ironed. This man wore his hair in a queue under a cap and dressed in a long Chinese robe. Young boys in the neighborhood would often chase him as he made his deliveries, yelling vulgar names at him.

One day, there was a knock on her grandmother's kitchen door, and it was Mr. Yee with a huge bundle wrapped in newspaper. Her grandmother greeted him, "Oh, good morning, Mr. Yee. Won't you come in? Please sit down."

Mr. Yee handed her this large package and said, "This is for you." She opened it and inside there were two exquisite ancient Chinese vases. She said, "Oh, Mr. Yee, these are far too valuable. I could not accept them." Mr. Yee insisted that he wanted her to have them. She looked at him and said, "Mr. Yee, why do you want me to have your vases?"

He looked at her and a tear came down his cheek as he said, "Mrs. Wicks, I've been in this town for ten years. They won't let me bring my wife and children, so I am going back to China to be with them and the vases were all I brought with me. I want you to have them."

She looked at Mr. Yee and asked, "Mr. Yee, why do you want *me* to have your vases?" He looked at her with tears in his eyes and said, "Mrs. Wicks, I have been in this town for ten years and you are the only one who has ever called me, 'Mr. Yee.'"

One can imagine the insults and names that Mr. Yee was called in his ten years in that little mining town. So, when Hesselbein's grandmother told her that story, Hesselbein cried her heart out. She cried for poor Mr. Yee. When her grandmother died, she left a little card that said, "I want Frances to have Mr. Yee's vases." Today, they're in Hesselbein's living room, and every time she looks at the vases, she remembers her grandmother, Mr. Yee, and respect for all people.

Purpose Driven

In the early 1960s, as a mother of a little eight-year-old boy in a small steel mill community in western Pennsylvania, Hesselbein unexpectedly found herself the leader of Girl Scout Troop 17. A church-basement-based troop asked her to fill in as leader temporarily. With thirty ten-year-old girls under her supervision, Hesselbein took her first steps toward becoming an organizational leader.

Finding the work rewarding, Hesselbein continued volunteering for the next eight years, working with the same group of girls until they graduated from high school. During this time, she was recruited to be the executive director of the local Girl Scouts council, then of the Girl Scouts of Western Pennsylvania. And that's when Hesselbein needed to define leadership for herself.

She began implementing the principles of the father of modern business management, Peter Drucker, who later became a close partner and valued advisor of the organization. To effectively lead, Hesselbein learned that you must first have a mission that you're passionate about because it is the fundamental purpose of the work. Mission forms a point of true connection with people. It's about distilling the language. The mission must be concise enough "to fit on a T-shirt," as Drucker often touted. In the case of the Girl Scouts, that mission became firmly entrenched:

"To help each girl reach her own highest potential."

"Whether you're the president of a Girl Scout council or you're the CEO of the largest organization for girls and women in the world, it doesn't matter," says Hesselbein. "Somehow, in doing your work, you must create meaning around your purpose."

Hesselbein has found that the most successful corporations understand the power of their mission and they use it. They don't just have values—they live them. A mission may change over time, as the goals of the organization change to meet the changing needs of the organization. But at the end of the day, "We need to make those words count," urges Hesselbein.

It is through this dedication to creating a powerful mission statement, and other powerful writing, that Hesselbein caught the attention of the national organization and was invited to become the national executive director of the Girl Scouts of the USA in 1976. She landed the position and served as the organization's leader for the next thirteen years, transforming how the organization attracted and embraced new members.

From Mission to Action

Rising from volunteer troop leader to CEO of the Girl Scouts of the USA, Hesselbein made every effort to turn the organization's mission into action. With an underlying purpose of "building girls of courage, confidence, and character, who make the world a better place," Hesselbein knew the organization needed to invest in training its leaders to deliver on its promise of helping each girl reach her own highest potential.

This is not a one-time training event either. Continuing

professional education of leaders at every level is essential to learning and growing. Hesselbein also pushed to expand its membership and become a more inclusive organization. She has been heralded for increasing membership among minorities, creating the Daisy Scouts for five-year-olds, addressing social issues impacting children, and creating new badges for modern skills.

Recognizing that times do, indeed, change, Hesselbein emphasizes that organizations must also evolve to meet the needs of the people they serve. Leaders should keep checking to ensure that their mission aligns with the current challenges facing the organization, its people, and the communities it serves.

Bringing People Together

In 1976, Hesselbein also became the first woman in the U.S. to be invited to chair a United Way campaign, unbeknownst to her at the time. After recognizing how much money Hesselbein helped the Girl Scouts raise, she was asked to be the chairman. And, as chairman, she was able to choose a vice chairman, who would become chair the following year.

She selected the president of the local United Steel Workers as her vice chairman. Hesselbein recalls the bewilderment of the committee upon announcing her selection. She also went a step further and said that she would like the national president of the American Federation of Labor and Congress of Industrial Organizations (AFLCIO) to do the kickoff with her.

For the first time, due to Hesselbein's selection, both organized labor and big corporations were intentional partners bonded by active support of the United Way campaign. And that year, little Johnstown, Pennsylvania had the highest per capita giving of any United Way in the USA. By engaging everyone in the campaign, it became a huge success.

In a hundred years, there have been only two women to chair a United Way campaign in the world. It wasn't until a recent article in the *New York Times* announced the second woman chair, that Hesselbein learned she was indeed the first in 1976. The second, in New York City in 2018.

It's About the People

It's important to find the people who are making the greatest difference, not just repeating the past, when looking for mentors and partners in business. According to Hesselbein, "If leadership is a matter of how to be, then it's important to find great people who were making such a difference." And Hesselbein recognizes how fortunate the Girl Scouts organization was for having such great people wanting to work with them.

Among many others, she has come to view the former CEO of the Ford Motor Company, Alan Mulally, as one of those people. Mulally is recognized as a leader who looks to his people and gives them respect and appreciation. Hesselbein recalls one specific incident that exemplified Mulally as a person of character. Hesselbein held a two-year chair for the study of leadership at West Point and would teach a class of twenty-four cadets every other month. She thought it would benefit the cadets if she brought with her a great thought leader to join each discussion. She invited Mulally to be one of those speakers.

Hesselbein recalls introducing Mulally as "a great corporate leader in America who is famous for transforming the Ford Motor Company." Mulally looked at the students, and in a very serious voice said, "I did not transform the Ford Motor Company. The people of Ford transformed the Ford Motor Company."

Cheering erupted from the class of cadets. This correction of Hesselbein's introduction to include his people in his success was inspiring for everyone in the room to witness firsthand. It is through this kind of transparent and genuine recognition of others that Hesselbein believes leaders motivate and inspire people to take meaningful action.

To Serve Is to Live
There have been two institutions that have sustained our democracy, according to Hesselbein. One is the public school system. When thinking about the beginning of our country, the public schools were influential to all the children, especially the poor and underserved children. It is from the support of the community, teachers, and monetary contributions that the public school system has survived all these years to generate countless evidence of ongoing improvement. The United States Army is the other institution that she believes has sustained our democracy. It is through the efforts of dedicated soldiers who sacrifice their time (and life) to serve our country has survived and prospered.

In Hesselbein's eyes, "To serve is to live." We must always seek opportunities to serve and support others. In that regard, Hesselbein believes that we should respect the views of protestors.

"Whether you stand up, or sit down, or lie down, we have to be able to say to protestors, 'We appreciate the way you feel,'" says Hesselbein. "I think respect for all people has to be the most powerful message."

It is this underlying respect for others in spite of any differences that creates an inclusive environment—one that unifies instead of alienates.

A Bright Future

While we've made great progress in terms of diversity and inclusion in our society, it's not enough according to Hesselbein. There is more that needs to be done. Leaders need to ensure that the people they want to attract and retain can find themselves inside organizations. They must be able to look at the board of directors, leaders, and employees, and find themselves. There needs to be a variety of perspectives and backgrounds represented.

While there is still room for improvement, Hesselbein sees a bright future ahead. Research studies have shown that millennials are more like those born in the 1930s and 1940s than any cohort since. Those individuals during that era were called "the greatest generation," which leaves Hesselbein feeling very positive about the future and the young people who will eventually lead the country.

For instance, she recalls a specific incident involving a few millennials who were part of the University of Pittsburgh's Hesselbein Global Academy for Student Leadership and Civic Engagement. After Hesselbein issued an open invitation to visit her office, a few students took her up on her offer and booked the first flight out the next morning and showed up in New York to spend the day there. While caught completely off guard, Hesselbein and her team threw out everything they had planned and spent the day with those young men and women.

"You know, there is something about right now—whether here or abroad—something about the millennials," says Hesselbein. "They're so inspiring. And the way they're volunteering all over the world—it's just so beautiful—so incredible. So, 'bright future' is my battle cry."

With such insight into what makes a leader effective, Hesselbein has shown us that purpose drives results because "achieving results without a mission is meaningless." Effective leadership comes from within and that purpose propels us forward—into a more fruitful tomorrow.

LEADERSHIP LESSON

As you reflect on her wisdom, consider your responsibilities as a leader and answer the "Five Most Important Questions" Hesselbein developed with Drucker:

What is your mission?

Who are your customers?

What do your customers value?

What are your results?

What is your plan?

NANCY SINGER

Author Introduction

If you accept the premise that ability is a function of task-specific knowledge, experience, and skill, we suggest for the task of developing global leaders, Nancy Singer has been a long-standing member of an elite group of cutting-edge learning professionals! She completed a distinguished career in the pharmaceutical industry, recently retired, and continues to contribute to the advancement of effective leadership practice as an executive coach, mentor, and consultant.

Singer's guiding principle: Stay true to your core values. She has been a lifelong student of leadership theory, practice, transfer, and impact. She intentionally had the kind of career that systematically combined rotations through operational roles in sales, marketing, and people management with positions in learning, training, and change management as well. Those jobs also featured experience with large, global, industry-leading entities, as well as ground-floor involvement with organizations that were literally just opening their doors.

When Singer was one of the original employees at a pharmaceutical startup, she built the sales training department (brick by brick), which entailed everything from designing a new training program for all professional sales representatives to creating a founding directors leadership forum. She also initiated a national call center, designing it from the ground up. Her natural creative abilities afforded her a unique opportunity to leave her stamp on what would become a much-admired pharmaceutical giant.

In general terms, her multiple transitions into leadership training roles provided her with the chance to immerse herself in learning and exploration of leadership constructs as well as methodologies for effective deployment. As a result, she developed what could best be described as an encyclopedic level of understanding and depth in the realm of leadership development.

That, in combination with a career full of opportunities to put theory into practice as a line manager and executive, produced a leader that could be counted upon to deliver targeted results and drive employee engagement. For example, when you ask people to recount their most awkward moments in leadership, you get a variety of different responses, of course, but one that you hear about with some degree of regularity is: a big promotion. You interviewed for a position of significance ... and got it ... but will be managing somebody that interviewed for the same position and didn't.

Most in those circumstances figure out a way to muddle through a difficult conversation or two as they assume their new role and stumble forward. Given that Singer's core values include honest and open communication, seeking feedback, and treating others with respect, she figured out a way to turn that discussion it into a source of energy for the individual in question, as well as an extended team of learning professionals, who would go on to design, develop, and deliver global, world-class, award-winning training for leaders at all levels.

Throughout the years Singer also refined her ability to conduct courageous conversations—the ones that most people will look for any excuse to avoid. Her skill for delivering candid and objective feedback while keeping a person "whole" led to breakthrough changes in the behavior and performance of her teams. Those changes had a direct, positive impact on productivity, morale, and retention. She was also defined by her willingness to take the time to mentor young managers in the hope of helping them sharpen this skill as well.

With all of that as background, Singer has a special place in her heart for women leaders. She grew up in a generation that featured very few females as leadership role models. Women struggled to get "a seat at the table," and when they finally did, found themselves in relative isolation. In many respects, she has made it her mission to forge a path for women leaders of the future and ensure they have equal and adequate resources and support.

"Core values act as a personal North Star."

- Nancy Singer

LEVERAGING YOUR CORE VALUES

Nancy Singer

Values-Based Leadership

Every person is driven by a unique set of values that influence their behavior, choices, and the direction of their lives. These principles become the foundation of your leadership. Aligning your personal values with your leadership goals provides leaders with an unwavering guide as they encounter challenges throughout their career.

"Core values act as a personal North Star," says Nancy Singer, founder and chief executive officer of Singer Leadership Group. "They help guide you in every decision you need to make when you come to forks in the road," she says. Knowing what is most important to you makes you better equipped to evaluate opportunities and how to handle conflicts when they arise.

Our values ground us as individuals and keep us focused on the things that matter. By integrating our personal values into our leadership strategy, leaders can form a more authentic connection with their employees, peers, and themselves.

Drive and Ambition

"Regardless of your intentions, leadership is about how other people perceive you and whether they will follow you or not," says Singer. No one is born a leader. It takes drive, ambition, and a willingness to be open to feedback and changing your behavior to be an extraordinary leader. It took time for Singer to realize that a leader is not necessarily the person who is taking center stage and giving the inspirational speech. A leader can influence outcomes from behind the scenes or even the sidelines.

Singer worked closely with a senior leader in human resources at Merck who showed her a different way to lead. Affectionately known as the "executive whisperer," this leader did not have the top title and was not the one who was often on center stage. And yet, Singer was struck by her credibility, power to influence, and ability to cause change, thereby impacting results, mostly from behind the scenes.

This led to an interesting pivot in Singer's life, causing her to consider how she might lead from a different place. She spent years at center stage and loved it, but she wanted to influence and change people from a different perspective. Her success at this put Singer on the path of becoming responsible for all leadership development around the world at Merck.

Another learning, early in Singer's career, was understanding the value of cultivating her peer-to-peer influencing skills. Great leaders achieve results through other people, not just their subordinates. While Singer admires individuals who have the drive and ambition to take chances and innovate, she would quickly lose patience with those who lacked these characteristics and sometimes essentially write them off. This would prove disadvantageous when she needed to work with them.

By refocusing on her core values, self-reflection, and opening herself up to hearing feedback from some wise and caring managers, she strengthened her peer-to-peer interpersonal skills. As a result, her professional network expanded, and all parties benefitted from improved relationships.

Women's Leadership Development

As a senior executive in global leadership development at Merck, Singer developed many flagship programs that boosted the skills and engagement of employees across the organization. Specifically, Singer was approached by a colleague to develop a program targeted to increase the number of women in leadership roles at the company. At that point, most senior positions at the company were held by men.

To better understand why the leadership staff was predominately male, Singer and her team conducted a thorough analysis. The findings revealed that women were relatively unknown to the men who were making the hiring decisions. In other words, women didn't network or brand themselves as well as their male colleagues, and they needed help to increase their confidence and executive presence.

Committed to increasing the number of women in leadership positions at the company, Singer and her team partnered with Simmons College, an all-female college in Boston, to develop a women's leadership development program.

The program focused on branding, networking, influencing, and helping women develop more self-awareness—all the leading reasons women were not being promoted at Merck. Singer pushed to include men in the program. "Women have to work with men. Men have to work with women," says Singer. "I really wanted to involve men to help open doors for these women."

Each program invited four or five male allies who would listen to the experiences of the female employees. During the program, each woman shared their leadership journey and the challenges they had encountered. The men were instructed not to problem solve; rather, just listen. That evening, the men each dined with a small group of women to discuss what was happening at the company relative to women's issues and how they might create change. Small projects and initiatives were identified and implemented with the support of these male allies, and the culture relative to the female experience slowly changed.

The immersive, two-day experience helped increase awareness of women's issues and fostered new relationships among the participants and senior executives, which increased the familiarity of male executives with potential female successors for senior-level roles.

This program has been in place for over ten years and contributed to increasing the number of women in leadership positions. While there is still room for improvement in creating a more balanced leadership team, the program has helped to close the gender gap at Merck and bring more women into executive and c-suite positions.

The Future of Leadership

Singer believes that, as we move to an increasingly virtual workforce, building effective and efficient teams will be a crucial component of business success. "Historically, in almost any industry or corporation, big or small, we get most of our work done through teams," notes Singer. "Unfortunately, paying attention up front to team dynamics and basic operating guidelines often gets ignored in service of 'moving forward quickly.' In fact, this can have just the opposite effect."

Singer believes that teams are more effective if they take time when forming or onboarding new members to get to know each other, discuss the type of team they want to be, how they will behave with each other, set communication and meeting protocols, establish how decisions will be made, and how they will resolve conflict. Ignoring these preliminaries puts teams at risk of getting stuck, having difficulty overcoming obstacles, and not resolving the natural conflict that arises among people who impact engagement and results. Work should be fun. It rarely happens that way just organically; you need to be intentional about it.

The need for operationally efficient teams will greatly expand in the future. As tomorrow's work environment becomes more and more impacted by the evolution of technology and geographically dispersed employees, tomorrow's leaders will need to connect, influence, and inspire teams from afar in this digital space. Organizations that fail to invest the time or resources into developing strong and resilient teams risk losing a real competitive advantage.

As the business world continues to evolve, leaders must remain resilient and adaptive to change. By tapping into the core values, leaders are equipped to connect with others and navigate unforeseen challenges together—now and in the future.

LEADERSHIP LESSON

List your core values.

Create a North-Star statement based on your values.

How do you want to be perceived as a leader?

What kind of working environment do you want to create for your teams and colleagues?

Why? What outcomes do you hope to achieve through your work?

Identify developmental goals.

Identify specific actions you can take that will bridge gaps between the current state and your ideal state, reflected in your North-Star statement. Monitor your progress every few months.

PATRICK STOKES

Author Introduction

We imagine there are several people we have interviewed for this book that you have certainly heard of or perhaps about which you have even already read something. We would further imagine that Patrick Stokes probably isn't one of those people. And, as long as we are surmising things, we're guessing there is a very strong probability that somewhere along the way a "Patrick-Stokes-like character" played a significant role in formulating the direction of your path in life.

Stokes is a high school history teacher and football coach at Eastern Alamance High School in Mebane, North Carolina. When asked to estimate the number of kids he has impacted during his fifteen-year tenure in that dual capacity, he pauses because it is clear it is not a question he was anticipating or a topic he may have ever considered. He eventually responds by saying, "I guess I'd have to say ... several thousand."

Almost the exact minute he says that, you find yourself thinking: I wonder how many other Stokes-like teachers and coaches there are who quietly and effectively influence kids navigating the terrain between adolescence and adulthood.

The answer you come up with is: Thankfully, quite a few, but regrettably ... nowhere near enough!

Further, when you ask most people how they wound up "doing what they are doing" you frequently get answers that highlight a series of almost random transitions:

> "I started out doing this and wound up there; then I did that for a while and figured out it really wasn't my thing. So, then I sort of fell into this other deal and really like it! We'll see where things go from *here!*"

Not so for Stokes! He can tell you, with unmistakable passion in his eyes, the exact moment in time he knew precisely what he wanted to do with his life. He was fifteen years old. He was jumping around a locker room with a few dozen teammates after a victory of significance. In so doing they were honoring their coach, who was a fair-but-firm role model, who had taught them so very many important lessons about life:

- hard work and sacrifice
- the importance of having a purpose, or a goal, or some type of noteworthy objective that demands focused attention
- the power and corresponding potential of transparent camaraderie and peer accountability
- the uninhibited and undeniable pure joy you feel when you accomplish that objective of significance and make the people you care most about in the world so very, very proud—right there; right then!

Stokes knew he wanted to help kids of the future feel what he was feeling at that very moment.

So, Stokes teaches history and he coaches football. Each year he is an active part of a faculty that greets three hundred or so fourteen-year-old students. Those kids are going to change immeasurably during their tenure at East Alamance, and you can just tell that Stokes is the kind of teacher/coach that is going to do everything he can possibly do to help guide those transitions. He tells you how he "watches kids": how they integrate into new and intimidating circumstances, how they handle success, how they handle setbacks, and how they help (or don't help) the kids less talented or less fortunate than they are. The distant and intentional observation of those dynamics, ultimately, helps him help them.

Of course, each year inevitably also includes a graduation ceremony. Three hundred or so eighteen-year-olds with a cap and a gown walking across a stage to head off into whatever the future may bring. And you can't help but think those that had the opportunity to be influenced by Stokes are far more prepared for that future than they would have been otherwise, even if some or perhaps even many don't fully recognize it at the time.

"If you don't have a system in place, then you have nothing in place."

— Patrick Stokes

SETTING THE TONE

Patrick Stokes

It Starts with Structure

Whether it's in business, politics, coaching, or teaching, we're all searching for the same things: love, passion, and leadership.

Even leaders are looking for leadership or some semblance of direction. As a seasoned high school history teacher and football coach in North Carolina, Patrick Stokes has learned the importance of having a plan both on and off the football field.

"If you don't have a system in place, then you have nothing in place," says Stokes. As a young teacher, Stokes learned the value of setting the tone by creating a framework of rules that should be adhered to as strictly as possible.

"Without a plan, there is a lack of structure and people are naturally going to test their boundaries. Leaders must clearly articulate a core set of values and hold others accountable if they fail to maintain those standards. As time goes on and you begin to understand the people with whom you're working, you can make exceptions based on their character. But, initially, you need to protect the integrity of what it is you're representing," says Stokes.

Laying the Groundwork

Stokes first learned the meaning of leadership from his high school football coach. When Stokes was fourteen years old, the summer before freshman year, he recalls running late for the first team meeting of the season. Walking into the meeting five minutes late, the coach stopped and told him to sit outside because the meeting had already started.

Stokes sat in the hallway for an hour, nervously wondering what the coach was going to say to him. Afterward, the coach gave him a lecture about the importance of being on time and how tardiness would not be tolerated. Accepting his punishment, Stokes did a few extra runs at the start of practice and never forgot the importance of punctuality.

That moment was not only impactful for himself, but also for the team. By having a zero-tolerance policy for tardiness and holding Stokes accountable for being late, the coach set the tone and shaped the mindset of the team. It created an environment where every player needed to be present and ready to work. They were all accountable to each other to perform to the best of their ability—nothing less. This tactic worked because Stokes' coach led the team to a state championship his senior year of high school.

Having a common goal brings focus to a diverse group of people because everyone is there for the same reason. Regardless of race, gender, money, status, or opinions, differences do not matter on the playing field. The only thing that matters is winning—the shared goal.

But, to achieve success, leaders must have a plan in place to effectively lead people. Stokes leads by three rules:

1. We are going to do the right thing.
2. We are going to make the most of the opportunities that we're given.
3. We are going to respect and love each other.

"If you follow those three rules, the rest of it kind of takes care of itself," says Stokes. These rules provide a foundation that his students and players need to make good decisions and to be successful.

Servant Leadership

"Being a leader does not mean you are the boss; it simply means that you're helping someone else," explains Stokes. A leader can be anyone—a child who helps another student unprompted, a mother encouraging her children, or a person holding a door open for a stranger.

Servant leadership is at the heart of being a teacher and coach. Whether it's providing an education or character development on the football field, they are selling a product to both the students and their parents, and they are expected to deliver the very best product that they can.

To successfully develop others, leaders must understand how to connect with people. Everyone is unique in how they feel acceptance and love. For some people, gifts or words of kindness resonate well, while other people feel valued from a handshake. A high five to one person may mean more than a hundred positive words of encouragement. Identifying how to connect with people enables you to become a better leader. This process helps to build trust so that you can take people to the places that they need to go, believes Stokes.

Being of service to other people is what motivates Stokes. "If you're not motivated naturally showing up, then that's a problem," he explains. A lack of motivation is going to negatively impact your performance and ultimately lead to poor results and outcomes. Finding passion and purpose in your work is critical to maintaining motivation and drive.

While teaching and coaching may not be glamorous in the financial sense, there is fulfillment in enabling the success of other people. To truly be effective, leaders must put their own expectations and self-interest aside and focus on the success of the individual. The best and worst part about being a teacher is the ticking time clock. "Every year there's a new batch of kids," explains Stokes. "Teachers and coaches have a four-year window to develop these kids, and while you may have the best of intentions, you're not going to be able to reach them all. As disappointing as that may be, you can't get discouraged."

Just like other companies and corporations, teachers and coaches have stakeholders too—parents. Meeting the expectations of parents is a challenge because every parent is advocating for their own child. Everybody wants to play. Everybody wants to be in the spotlight. And parents get very passionate about their kids. When this happens, coaches must reiterate the team rules to the parents and if they don't like those rules, then their child doesn't have to play. That may not be what the parent wants to hear, but at the end of the day, you've got to do what's best for the team, believes Stokes.

It's the team unit that matters most. One athlete doesn't win a game. It takes dedication and commitment from the entire team to lead to success. Everyone needs to show up motivated to work toward the goal. There are no exceptions. Even those individuals who show extreme promise and "superstar" potential are not exempt from following the rules. "Just because you have talent doesn't give you a get-out-of-jail-free card," explains Stokes. Keeping the kids grounded in the three core values helps him navigate through those challenging situations.

Great Leaders

When looking for leadership inspiration, Stokes, a history teacher, naturally reflects on historical leaders who have demonstrated admirable behavior and qualities. Teddy Roosevelt is one figure who comes to mind as exhibiting passion, charisma, and the ability to take chances. Stokes admires the risks and spirit of Teddy Roosevelt despite the negative traits he may have possessed.

"Then, on the other side, Teddy's distant cousin, Franklin Roosevelt, is a testament of true character," says Stokes. Franklin Roosevelt was a victim of polio and wheelchair bound, undergoing significant bullying throughout his childhood. Facing so much adversity in his own life and in the face of the greatest economic disaster America will hopefully ever see, Roosevelt still believed that, "The only thing we have to fear is fear itself." He didn't just passively believe that, he had a plan. In the first 100 days, he did more than any other president in the life of the administration.

Stokes also admires our first president of the United States,

George Washington, not just as a military leader but more as a manager of people. When you sit back and think about it, Washington had to manage all the great leaders of our country. He had very influential leaders in his cabinet: James Madison, Thomas Jefferson, Alexander Hamilton, and John Adams. The way he managed his team was amazing to Stokes.

There were countless other leaders from his history books that Stokes admired. People like Betty Friedan, Gloria Steinem, and John Lewis had courage. They were willing to shake up the foundation of our nation to do what they felt was right. To do the right thing. "They didn't just talk it," says Stokes. "They walked it. They lived it. They were people of action."

Stokes may not have agreed with all the actions of these historical leaders, but that's not the point. These were people who acted honorably in the face of opposition. They developed a plan in the midst of chaos. And they brought people together.

Managing Success

Stokes doesn't often stop to smell the roses and enjoy his victories. He handles success much like he handles failures—with a lot of personal reflection on how he can improve and make things better.

"When it comes down to it, a ballgame is just a ballgame," says Stokes. "When it's with your students or your own children, you might not get tomorrow to leave an impression."

Parenting is a juggling act of responsibilities. It's about making decisions in the moment and deciding how much to insert yourself into a situation. Sometimes children need you to step in and advocate for them. Other times, they need you to step aside and let them handle the situation. There are moments when they need tough love, and then there are times when they need understanding and compassion.

"You don't know how it's going to play out, but you'd better be prepared to make the best decision possible at that moment," says Stokes. "Otherwise, you're going to lose and you're going to miss out."

Success doesn't come easy. As a leader (parent, teacher, coach, etc.), you must hold yourself accountable to your core values, and Stokes does just that. He lives by his three rules: do the right thing, make the most of what you're given, and respect and love others.

Stokes has been a successful high school football coach for fifteen years, winning at least ten regular season games during that timeframe. Despite the success, he remains grounded, realizing the grass isn't always greener on the other side. For him, it's not about title or position or chasing fame and money, it's about doing the best that he can with what he has been given in the moment. It's not about settling or complacency; it's about evaluating your situation and, ultimately, deciding where you're needed most. And for Stokes, he's right where he needs to be.

LEADERSHIP LESSON

How old were you when you figured out what
you wanted to do with your life professionally?

What factors contributed to that decision?

Based on your experience, what is the
relationship between passion and purpose?
What about motivation and drive?

What could you do, specifically, to recognize
or show appreciation to a teacher or coach
like Patrick Stokes in your community or from
your past?

JIM YONG KIM

Author Introduction

There has long been a spirited debate regarding whether leaders are born or made. Stated differently:

- Are there certain innate characteristics or attributes that distinguish leaders from the rest of us? Or ...

- Is leadership a skill that can be broken down into interdependent subsets, practiced and improved upon?

Not surprisingly, after careful review, we would suggest the answer to those questions is ... yes! Consider Dr. Jim Yong Kim in that context. Dr. Kim is a Korean-born physician and anthropologist who, among many other things, was the twelfth president of the World Bank. In 2013, he was listed by *Forbes Magazine* as one of the most powerful people on the planet. His talent was also on active display for all to see from a very early age.

He immigrated to the United States when he was five and grew up in a town called Muscatine, Iowa. He was the valedictorian and president of his high school class and was also the quarterback of the football team and point guard for the basketball team. He graduated magna cum laude from Brown University with a BA in human biology before going on to receive his MD and PhD in anthropology from Harvard. He has published numerous articles in academic and scientific journals that spoke to his primary arena of expertise (infectious diseases including tuberculosis [TB] and HIV) and chaired several committees on global health policy.

When you have that kind of academic grounding in combination with the demonstrated ability to understand complex problems at a level that clearly separates you from the pack, what sort of challenges do you pursue? In Dr. Kim's case, it was the problems very few people in public health sought to address: major epidemics and pandemics like drug-resistant tuberculosis, HIV, and Ebola in developing countries. This led him, in 1987 with a handful of other talented partners, to form Partners in Health (PIH).

PIH began with a radical, innovative, and transformative approach to community-focused health care in Haiti. Protocols were designed for treating complex medical problems like drug-resistant tuberculosis through an approach that relied heavily on trained community health workers. While Haiti remains the largest program, today PIH has over 13,000 employees serving patients in twelve developing countries in Latin America, Africa, and countries of the former Soviet Union.

Not surprisingly his counsel has been in great demand of late. When you hear him address the "once-in-a-lifetime challenges" presented by the COVID-19 virus, you truly begin to appreciate the depth of his value as a global leader. He can break down the extremely complicated forces of virus-induced disruptive change in a manner that both instills hope and charts a course forward.

It is safe to say Dr. Kim has impacted millions of people around the world. Is he a special person with unique talent? Absolutely! Are there elements of his journey that can help the rest of us dream and then put that vision into action to make the world a better place? Without a doubt!

"Leadership is working with a group of people and helping them to do things that otherwise would never have been doable."

- Jim Yong Kim

UNLOCKING POTENTIAL WITH HUMILITY

Jim Yong Kim

The Power of Teams

Academia is often viewed—by both business leaders and academics—as the antithesis to industry. Even today, amid unprecedented collaboration between corporations and universities, the ivory tower stereotype persists as does the cynical view of industry being rife with corporate greed.

But the delineation between scholarship and business is an illusion—there is a crucial synergy between the two worlds. Jim Yong Kim, MD, PhD, knows this well, having spent phases of his long and varied career in each setting. In fact, Kim's studies in anthropology and his background as an Ivy League professor and president of Dartmouth directly informed his thinking about how to succeed in business environments.

Kim, who is now vice chairman and partner at private equity firm Global Infrastructure Partners, recalls studying the origins of human civilization. "I often wondered what it was that allowed the earliest humans to survive when the fauna around them were more powerful and had bigger teeth," he says.

Kim's answer is the basis for his vision of leadership. "This ability of people to work together so that they can accomplish things as teams that they never would've been able to accomplish individually—this is the task of leadership," he explains. "It's also the most fundamental trait of human beings that has enabled us to accomplish what we've accomplished."

In other words, leadership is a key to humans' place in the world today—a place where the seemingly impossible is achieved with striking regularity.

Charting the Course

Humanity's challenges today are much different—saber-toothed tigers are long-extinct—but the stakes are just as high. Our survival as a species is still dependent on the ability of groups to work together to solve problems, and how well we accomplish that is directly related to the type and quality of leadership available. "There's no question that it makes a huge difference," Kim emphasizes.

Leaders are responsible for mapping out an organizational direction and that begins with a vision. "You come in and set a bolder vision and support it with a set of clear, ethical, moral principles," says Kim. In turn, those principles drive the behavior of those in the organization and how you approach problems. "In the end, you accomplish so much more than any individual—or even smaller groups—could have accomplished on their own."

While there are many ways that a leader can inspire others to help them achieve their vision, there are only two directions for a leader to move an organization—toward goals or away from them. "With new leadership, an organization either gets better or it gets worse," Kim explains. "There are very few organizations that just keep going in the same direction with leader after leader."

Walking the Walk

Working with others to establish behavioral change is important—but it's not enough. Leaders must not only encourage but actively model the types of behavior that support their vision. Kim recalls one of his most influential leadership role models, Alan Mulally, as a striking example.

Kim describes Mulally as disciplined, brilliant, and compassionate. "But there are a lot of people who have those traits who don't bring them together in a form of leadership that's truly transformative," he says. To do that, leaders must truly embody those traits and behaviors they want individuals to exhibit. And that takes not only desire but also discipline.

Widely credited with transforming the Ford Motor Company from a mediocre business to one that enjoyed nearly twenty profitable quarters in a row, Mulally enacted an ambitious plan called One Ford—a plan to get disconnected, competing interests to work together across the company. And it worked. Why? "All of the traits that these legendary great leaders supposedly have, you could see that it wasn't fluff for Alan," says Kim. "He was committed to it. He was sincere about it."

Leaders must be disciplined enough to act in accordance with the rules—the codes of behavior—they've put in place to support their vision. "I was blown away by what Alan was doing [at Ford]," Kim says. "What I learned was that the level of discipline he had to make his plans happen, he just had to be at the core of it in order for it to work."

Always on Stage

Kim remembers one particular dinner where he asked Mulally for last words of advice. Responding to Kim and another colleague, Mulally said, "You guys both have really nice smiles. Use them more." When questioned further, Mulally continued, "If I walk out of Ford and I've got a frown on my face, you know what happens to the stock of Ford?" He was intimating that the rise and fall of fortunes occurred at the whim of his facial expressions.

Mulally knew that leaders are on stage—constantly. Of course, there are times that you feel negative, exasperated, or even angry. But it is crucial to differentiate between your emotions and your behavior. "If you are really serious about leadership, you must understand that your facial expressions are not your own anymore," Kim points out.

A leader has the responsibility to show the organization that "I'm up. I'm positive. I believe in my mission. I love what I'm doing. I have great faith in you," explains Kim. "That's a lesson that's just burned into my soul."

Play to Your Strengths

Most people—quite logically—strive to get better at what they're not good at and to improve their areas of weakness. But Kim discovered an alternative perspective that made sense to him. "I started reading the leadership literature and started thinking about how I could become a better leader," he says. "Leadership is getting better and better at what you're good at and simply managing those things that you're weak at," an insight he gleaned from the book *Soar with Your Strengths* by Don Clifton.

The best way for leaders to balance out their weaknesses is to surround themselves with people who can compensate for those shortcomings. "That was really helpful to me," Kim shares. "I'm not the best at managing the details of running something day to day. I always made sure that I found someone I trusted who would pay attention to the details. Then I would go off and do the things that I felt that I was strong at."

This lesson hit home during Kim's time at Partners in Health where he served as executive director from 1987-2003. "I'll never forget the clinicians that I would watch walk into a room, and the patient's face would light up." But while Kim was a compassionate clinician and a good teacher, he knew those were not his true strengths. "I needed to find something where I could bring everything I have to the table and feel that I'm being challenged and that I'm learning," Kim says. It was then that he started to form an interest in policy and the bigger public health issues surrounding what he was tackling at Partners in Health.

This new way of thinking formed a thread that would tie together Kim's many different careers—the notion of a preferential option for the poor. "I think the thing I'd like to be known for is that I found a principle," Kim explains. His mission wasn't loyalty to any one organization, he discovered, and his future careers would make that even clearer. His true mission was much bigger—to try to end poverty in the world.

Developing Leaders

"Identifying leaders is an art form that you have to approach with great humility," says Kim. Leaders who haven't put a lot of thought into leadership tend to bring with them stereotypes about who leaders should be and how they should behave. "So, you may miss the quiet young woman who doesn't always speak up in meetings but has an extraordinary ability to motivate and guide others," Kim notes.

"You have to be extremely humble and very self-conscious about how we all have a tendency to think about leadership in ways that are overly influenced by media images," he warns. You must "constantly question your own assumptions about what you think leadership really is."

Being open to coaching is another way leaders can examine their own assumptions. "In terms of developing leaders, I have become a huge believer in coaching," Kim says. "Even if there are people who are doing well, I always offer people leadership coaching so that they can do even better." That's also a way you can distinguish those with true leadership potential, according to Kim. "I think that's the most important part of leadership: if people are ready and willing to try to get better with each new challenge."

Kim warns against leaders who lack self-awareness. "If you don't have that basic commitment to humbly understand how others experience you and what the others would like you to do differently, think about doing something that doesn't require leadership," he advises.

You Must Eat the Sh--!

From layoffs at the World Health Organization to budget cuts at Dartmouth, Kim learned that, as a leader, you will not always be popular—but you must do what must be done. "The worst thing you can do as an incoming president is to make budget cuts the first item on the agenda," says Kim. "But there was no question that it had to be done, so I did it. It didn't make me popular with the faculty. It didn't make me popular with anybody."

Leading an organization means being fully committed to do what it takes to achieve success. That often means swallowing your pride and exhibiting a level of humility that can be achieved by few. This concept was described to Kim in a rather colorful manner by a colleague in a high-powered leadership group during Kim's time at the World Bank Group where he was president from 2012-19. When asked what he learned after a 360 review, the colleague replied, "I learned I must eat the sh--." This means that in order to be a good leader, you cannot set your own boundaries for how humble you need to be, Kim points out.

Kim recalls a memorable time he put this into practice. When he first started at the World Bank Group, he was greeted with a board of directors that he was told was going to be "his worst nightmare." Throughout his career, Kim had noted others' missteps, like immediately butting heads with the board or trying to go around them. But Kim, understanding that humility was so important, went on a charm offensive.

"I took them out for Korean food. We sang karaoke together. I spent time with them individually. I heaped praise on the board members for the many good things they did. No matter who they were or where they came from, there was always something remarkable about them that I could praise them for, and I always took the time to find out what that was."

Kim's lesson here is that if you are committed enough, you will do what it takes to achieve your organizations' goals, although many times it means putting yourself last. "If you really want to be a great leader, there can be no limit to the acts of humility that you're willing to take on," he says. "I've had my share of failures in leadership, and many of them occurred when I thought that it was OK to skip one or another act of humility."

A Simple Lesson
Kim recalls a research panel he participated in as part of the Gallup Leadership Institute early in his career. In it, a group of researchers interviewed high-performing, high-level managers and asked them why they left their jobs. The team expected answers about money or promotions. But it wasn't that. The interviewees consistently expressed the feeling that "nobody at that institution cared about me."

Of course, their supervisors had a completely different perspective when the information was brought back to them. "The supervisor would classically say, 'That's crazy.

That person was doing so well, I didn't have to spend any time with him or her at all,'" says Kim.

A leader has to care—not only about meeting objectives and achievements, but about people. And they have to show it in a way that their employees will understand. Again, Kim points to Mulally's influence. "This was the most accomplished CEO in the world, and he took the time to learn the janitors' names," Kim says. "He knew the name of every janitor that was cleaning that floor. He knew the name of the waitress who served us in the cafeteria."

The decision-makers aren't the only—or even the most important—people that a leader has to pay attention to. "I try to deeply understand not only who the decision-makers are but who the workers are and who my colleagues are. What do they want? What's at stake for them? Do I care enough to come up with an approach to leadership that will lift people up and draw from their strengths?" To Kim, this is what's at the core of a great leader.

LEADERSHIP LESSON

Consider the statements below and rate each based on your perception: 1—Unsure; 3—Maybe; 5—Absolutely.

The people I lead are aware of how valuable they are.

The people I lead are aware of how much I care about them.

Identify specific actions you can take to ensure the people you lead understand their value and know how much you care.

What are your greatest strengths as a leader?

What actions can you take to further leverage those strengths and improve your ability to effectively influence others?

ALAN MULALLY

Author Introduction

In a word, Alan Mulally is *special*. With an aeronautical engineering degree from the University of Kansas, his accomplishments over thirty-seven years at The Boeing Company are legendary, and his tenure as the CEO of the Ford Motor Company from 2006-14 will forever define his impact as a leader.

Mulally's leadership at Ford is well-chronicled. When he assumed the reins, Ford was in a downward spiral that is still difficult to wrap your head around. The stock was trading at $1 per share, the company was going to post a loss of $17 billion (the worst in its 103-year history), and worldwide employee engagement/morale reflected that reality.

Mulally's first acts were to form a cohesive leadership team to understand and deal with business realities in a positive way and to come together around a compelling vision, comprehensive strategy, and relentless implementation process. He then convened a weekly meeting with the sixteen members of his leadership team. Initially, Mulally asked each of them to do two things:

1. Identify their strategy and plan to implement the vision.

2. Assess progress against the plan using the following guidelines:

    GREEN | On plan. Currently on target and projected to achieve goal.

    YELLOW | Not currently on plan but trending in a direction that would ultimately deliver desired results.

    RED | Not on plan and not sure how to get there, yet ... working on the better plan.

The results from that first meeting? Each of the sixteen team members reported GREEN even though the company they ran happened to be in a tailspin, headed toward a record $17-billion loss! Considering the impending reality, Mulally encouraged his team, "Let's do it again."

Eventually, a member of the executive team finally said, "RED!" He then went on to candidly describe a problem of significance with no real strategy to fix it.

Looking back, Mulally viewed this as one of the most important moments in the turnaround of Ford. In response to the transparent assessment, Mulally stood up and applauded. He offered congratulations for the courage to openly admit the problem—and even more—to admit that there was no real idea on how to solve it.

Mulally then said something few leaders have the nerve to say in the presence of their leadership teams: "OK ... we have a 'RED!' Above all else, sincere thanks for the transparency! Also, please recognize this ... it's OK!

Now, just to be clear, I don't have the answer either. But, good news! We have thousands of very smart people who work here at Ford. Let's get to work and find somebody who can help solve this problem."

What happened? The team turned their attention to the problem and identified people who had the experience and expertise to help. Within a few minutes, there was noticeable movement in a positive direction. What followed were a series of bold and effective decisions that drove a truly legendary transformation.

Mulally retired in 2014 with a 91% employee approval rating, which to our knowledge is unprecedented. During that year, Ford earned $7.2 billion, which translated to record profit-sharing bonuses of approximately $9,000 per employee.

So, what can we learn from this historic example and legendary leader? As we believe the pages that follow will indicate—plenty!

Among many other things, leaders should leverage facts and data to create a transparent environment where people own their readiness to perform. As Mulally said often, "The facts and data will set us free!" Beyond that, leadership is about discipline; cadence; and relentless, ongoing calibration. Having the ability to formulate a vision and motivate people to see that future state is important. But, at the end of the day, to be a leader, you need to create a culture of "Working Together©" to relentlessly implement the plan and continuously develop the better plan!

"Leadership is the personal, positive influence we have by being and doing."

- Alan Mulally

TO SERVE IS TO LIVE
Alan Mulally

Work Is Love Made Visible—To Serve Is to Live

As a young man, Alan Mulally's goals were simple: buy himself a pair of Levi's jeans, Weejuns shoes (the original penny loafers), *maybe* a car, and someday go to college. Today, he is known as "The Man Who Saved Ford," credited with leading the once-struggling auto company through one of the biggest business comebacks in corporate history. His secret? "I was taught, I learned, and I appreciated that to serve is to live," he says.

From his door-to-door paper routes to his lawn mowing business and bagging groceries at Dillons grocery store, Mulally found that providing a service that people appreciated—and that he was paid for—was not only fun, but deeply gratifying. He thrived on the "thank yous" and making a positive difference in people's everyday lives. This tenet of service to others would guide Mulally throughout his career, yielding impressive results during his time with The Boeing Company (where he was hired fresh out of college and eventually named CEO of Boeing Commercial Airplanes and president of Boeing Information, Space, and Defense Systems) and as CEO of the Ford Motor Company.

Service is a key component of leadership for Mulally, who defines leadership as "helping others come together around service to deliver a compelling vision that benefits all of the stakeholders for the greater good." Service is also a part of his legacy: "I hope that, in a small part, I'm remembered that I believed in service and the 'Working Together' principles, practices, and management system to deliver it," he says.

First, Be. Then, Do.

Frances Hesselbein's teachings on "being" helped shape Mulally's perspective on leadership. "Because you're a leader," he explains, "who you are has a tremendous influence on all the people that you interface with." Hesselbein, especially, embodies this concept for Mulally. "When you're around her, you don't want to let her down, but even when you're not around her, you don't want to let her down." An effective leader motivates others to do their best work—out of desire, not out of fear or obligation. "You're an inspiration. You're somebody to learn from," he points out.

Leaders should use self-reflection and awareness to continuously reevaluate who they are and how that affects the people around them, Mulally recommends. A leader's ability to influence, help, coach, and facilitate is very dependent on who that leader is as a person, he explains. "Where are you with regard to humility, love, service, and inclusion in both your competencies and your character?" he asks. "Leadership is who you are; what you do and how you do it will have the most significant impact on your leadership effectiveness and team performance," Mulally says.

"Working Together" for the Greater Good

Leadership plays an important role in every organization. The leader pulls everyone else together and rallies them around not only the organization's vision, but the leadership team's strategy and plan for achieving that vision. "The more you can understand how leadership contributes to the goals and objectives of the organization—the greater good—the better you're going to be at helping everybody to fit in, participate, and bring their best selves," Mulally explains.

The ability to work well with others enables a leader to adapt in a rapidly changing world. He cites his parents as key figures who taught him the importance of working together. Mulally recalls his mother's advice: "If you learn how to work together with other talented people, you're going to be able to make a significant and positive difference for the greater good worldwide."

This advice served Mulally well throughout his career. In fact, the most significant part of Mulally's plan for turning around the failing Ford Motor Company centered on people. People who, up until that point, were unable—and at times unwilling—to work together effectively. Again, his parents proved a powerful example. "My parents always invited the university students from around the world to Thanksgiving and Christmas [celebrations], because many times they couldn't go home," he remembers. "I got a chance to see, experience, and learn from diversity of thoughts and experiences; it was a window to the world."

That outlook helped him unite the various factions at Ford. "If we can get people together, we find out that what we have in common outweighs our differences," he says. "Then, we get a chance to decide whether we want to work together for the greater good." In Mulally's case, the greater good wasn't making the best airplanes, cars, and trucks in the word. It was about safe and efficient transportation and what that enables—bringing people together.

Cultivate Awareness

"I knew after a while that leadership was really important, and [leaders] really can make a big difference," Mulally recounts. "I was getting a chance to feel that myself, so I was even more committed to help others move forward on that journey also." Awareness is a key part of identifying and developing new leaders. Returning to his concept of "being," if a leader practices self-awareness and also has that same awareness of everyone that they're dealing with, they will be able to see where all of those people fall on that continuum of leadership development, Mulally explains.

From there, leadership development is a mix of putting those people in situations where they can get leadership experience and receive feedback, formal coaching, and education. "Everyone should have a personal, leadership, and working-together development plan, using not only their coach, but all the rest of their team. Mulally points to executive coach Marshall Goldsmith's Stakeholder Centered Coaching® as an invaluable tool in terms of a continuous improvement plan to develop leadership effectiveness. In Stakeholder Centered Coaching®, the stakeholders determine the degree of leadership improvement, in addition to the leadership coach and the person being coached.

Apply awareness not only to people, but to opportunities. "Everybody, when you're growing up, you think you've got to get to the answer really quick—follow your heart," Mulally says. But at that age, the majority of people aren't likely to know exactly what that means. Awareness is the answer. "If you are just aware, look at the opportunities, how it fits with service and what you care about, then you just keep following that process of awareness, seeking feedback, and understanding the opportunities to serve."

It Takes Courage

Effective leaders are very clear about the "culture," both the processes they'll use to accomplish an organization's objectives and the expected behaviors that everyone in the organization must adhere to. After all, it's behavioral change—in a positive direction—that ultimately allows an organization to move toward its goals. It's the leader's job to set, exhibit, nurture, and enforce those behaviors. And that takes courage.

The leadership role is very unique because only the leader can hold the team and all the stakeholders accountable for following the agreed-to "Working Together" culture, processes, and behaviors. The leader's contribution is to pull everybody together; hold themselves and everyone else accountable for the goals, objectives, and the behaviors set forth; and have zero tolerance for violating either. "It takes courage to lead this way and hold people accountable in a positive way," Mulally says.

Leadership hinges on working with people and that can be emotional, messy, and awkward, especially when those people aren't meeting the agreed-to culture expectations. Mulally recounts a conversation with best-selling author and organizational health expert Patrick Lencioni who lamented having tough conversations with people who weren't following the prescribed behaviors and processes. Lencioni saw it as a sacrifice and struggled with the reality of being a leader in those moments. "I never thought that was a sacrifice. I was serving, and it was needed, and it was OK to have those conversations and move on together," Mulally explains. "I don't think I'd ever be that way if I wasn't comfortable learning from everybody and also having the courage to commit to our working-together culture, processes, and behaviors."

Learn from Everyone

Even before he really understood what leadership was, Mulally was acutely aware of the leaders around him. "I'm very aware of the effect that people have on me," he says. From his parents, teachers, coaches, and faith leaders in his community, he was constantly observing. He was fascinated by the humility, love, service, and inclusion that those people presented. "I just couldn't get enough of observing leaders," he recalls. "I admired them. I wanted to know more about them, what they did, and how they did it."

But observing and learning from other leaders isn't just about finding positive role models. Through careful observation, a leader can learn not just who they want to emulate, but what kinds of behavior they want to avoid. "I've learned as much from 'negative' examples of leadership as I have from the positive examples," Mulally says. "Even leaders who only care about themselves and shareholder value—I've learned from them." It all ties into Mulally's core concept of being and doing. "It goes back to who you are, why you are that way, what you do, and how you do it. If you sort that out with every leader, you're going to learn a lot."

"I can't get enough of the less effective leaders and understanding where they're coming from," he says. It's been well-documented that the biggest problem everybody has in their organization—and one of the top reasons they eventually leave—is their boss. With an ineffective leader, the subordinates are "… stuck in the middle of this bureaucracy and they're playing politics. It's confusing and they're not authentic. They're scared." One of the best ways leaders can gauge their own effectiveness is to be aware of others' impact on themselves, and also be aware of their impact on others, Mulally explains. "Look into their eyes. Do they want to be with you? Do they want to work with you? Do they feel respected? Do they feel appreciated?"

Leader as Coach, Leader as Facilitator

According to Mulally, the leader's unique role is to pull everyone together around the organization's compelling vision for the organization, including the strategy and the plan for achieving that vision, and only the leader can hold everyone accountable to the fundamental "Working Together" principles and practices of how people in the organization will treat each other. The leader is no longer the subject matter expert; the leader's role has changed to coach and facilitator of functional and discipline experts.

"As a matter of fact," says Mulally, "whatever got you into the leader position is probably not going to be the thing that is going to be the biggest impact you're going to make. You're not now the subject expert of any one discipline. Your unique contribution now is to pull everybody together, holding yourself, your team, and all of the stakeholders accountable for the agreed-to 'Working Together' operating process, expected behaviors you're going to use, and organization results, with zero tolerance for violating either."

When the leader is fulfilling this role, you'll find a smart and healthy organization that is accomplishing its objectives with minimal politics and confusion. You'll see that everyone knows the plan, the areas that need special attention, and everyone is helping each other accomplish the plan and develop the better plan going forward by turning the REDs to YELLOWs to GREENs.

A Labor of Love

If Mulally's legacy could be described in any words other than "service," they would be "humility and love." "I'd be thrilled if I could be remembered for loving people, and that I cared about people," he says. To love and be loved— in that order—was the purpose of life, a tenant instilled in Mulally by his mother from an early age. "It wasn't about me," he says. "I just love people, even the ones that I don't agree with. I love helping people work together. I loved having the honor to learn and serve as their leader."

"Working Together," leading, serving—it's all about people and it's all about people working together. "Love them up," Mulally emphasizes. "We are creatures of God. We all have fundamental principles and practices about how we want to be treated and how we want to treat each other," he continues. This is how a leader creates a smart, healthy, and safe organization that minimizes politics and confusion and enables all the participants to bring their best selves to deliver the organization's compelling vision.

The most respectful thing a leader can do in their organization is to base their leadership on clarity, avoiding secrets, and ambiguity. "Share with everyone what the plan is. Share with them what the status is of every element of the plan. Respect them and listen to each other. Appreciate them, include them, and nurture our 'Working Together' principles, practices, and management system." That way, everybody knows the plan, the areas that need special attention, and everyone can help each other work together to deliver the organization's objectives for all the stakeholders and the greater good. At the most fundamental level, this is love. "When you lead with humility, love, and service, everybody is going to appreciate that," Mulally says. "And, they're going to lead with their best self. Don't you think?"

LEADERSHIP LESSON

Here is the "Working Together": Principles, Practices, and Management System developed by Mulally on the basis of his direct experience as a leader during his career at Boeing and Ford.

"Working Together": Principles, Practices, and Management System

Culture—Operating Process and Expected Behaviors

- People first ... love them up ♥
- Everyone is included
- Compelling vision, comprehensive strategy, and relentless implementation
- Clear performance goals
- One plan
- Facts and data
- Everyone knows the plan, the status, and areas that need special attention
- Propose a plan; positive, "find-a-way" attitude
- Respect, listen, help, and appreciate each other
- Emotional resilience—trust the process
- Have fun—enjoy the journey and each other

Alan

Consider the questions below and identify at least three specific actions you can take with members of your team to enhance their ability to work together more effectively:

Identify one specific action you can take to put **People First ... Love Them Up.** ♥

Identify one specific action you can take to ensure **Everyone is Included.**

Identify one specific action you can take to have a **Compelling Vision, Comprehensive Strategy, and Relentless Implementation.**

Identify one specific action you can take to have **Clear Performance Goals.**

Identify one specific action you can take to have
One Plan.

Identify one specific action you can take to have
Facts and Data.

Identify one specific action you can take to
ensure **Everyone Knows the Plan, the Status,
and Areas that Need Special Attention.**

Identify one specific action you can take to
**Propose a Plan; Positive, "Find-a-Way"
Attitude.**

Identify one specific action you can take to
**Respect, Listen, Help, and Appreciate
Each Other.**

Identify one specific action you can take to have
Emotional Resilience—Trust the Process.

Identify one specific action you can take
to **Have Fun—Enjoy the Journey and
Each Other.**

Identify three specific actions you can take to
Lead with Humility, Love, and Service.

Identify three specific actions you can take to
create our **"Working Together"** culture with
zero tolerance for violating the process and the
expected behaviors.

MADELEINE DEAN

An age-old debate in the field of leadership development concerns the nature of its origin:

Are leaders born or made?

In more explicit terms, is leadership an innate talent that organically blossoms with maturity or a skill set that aspiring leaders study, practice, and develop? While there are those that continue to adopt one position or the other, most stake out middle ground that can be encapsulated by some version of the following:

> Great leaders quite often possess distinctive characteristics that have been on active display as long as anyone can remember. As those leaders become aware of their gifts, they become dedicated students of influence, learning all they can from any available resource and elevating their proficiency as a result.

As much as anyone we have ever met, Madeleine Dean is a living, breathing example of that description in action!

She is one of seven children born to Bob and Mary Dean. When asked to identify her leadership role models, she says almost immediately and with the strongest possible conviction: my parents. It leaves you with a strong sense that whatever was going on in the Dean household a generation ago should have been captured and shared with the masses.

At the ripe old age of eighteen, she entered the world of politics, serving in an official capacity as a local committee person. After that, she headed off to college at La Salle where she graduated cum laude, and then to Widener University, where she earned her law degree. She met her husband, PJ Cunnane, along the way while working on a reelection campaign for a Pennsylvania state legislator by the name of Joe Hoeffel. She practiced law and taught English at La Salle University while she was raising her three sons.

When her children were grown, her political career kicked in with a flurry! She was elected township commissioner and soon thereafter (2012) became a state representative. As she describes her indoctrination to the State House, one cannot help but be reminded of what we all went through, in one version or another, on the first day of our freshman year in high school. That was where the seniors walked by our table in the lunchroom and put the word out that we'd better stay in line, know our place, and not speak unless we were spoken to! In her case, some ranking members of the Pennsylvania House approached her, congratulated her on her election, then strongly suggested she "say nothing … do nothing … and watch us." Predictably, although unexpectedly as far as the ranking members were concerned, she ignored the advice!

She dove into challenges like addiction prevention, equal rights, and gun violence. In the aftermath of Sandy Hook, she co-founded a gun violence prevention caucus with Pittsburg Representative Dan Frankel called PA SAFE. This, along with many other accomplishments during her tenure in the State House, fueled her election into the United States Congress in 2018 (one of four Pennsylvania women sent to Congress in that election and one of only seven women in history to represent the Keystone State in Washington).

Representative Dean remains an outspoken advocate for gun violence prevention, health care for all, education, ethical government, as well as the $15 minimum wage. She is both a member and a voice for the House Judiciary Committee and Financial Services Committee. As we believe you will soon find out, Dean is a born leader who continues to develop her leadership skill set to the benefit of us all.

"Leadership is made through circumstance, compassion, heart, passion and experience."

- Madeleine Dean

SPEAKING UP
Madeleine Dean

The Impact of Leadership Language

Being ethical and using sound judgment is at the fore of being a great leader. A leader knows when to speak up—whether it's to voice their opinion or when something is not quite right—and will use purposeful language to influence change.

Madeleine Dean, a member of the United State Congress, admires leaders who use their words to lift up other people. The most influential leaders craft smart, uplifting arguments that inspire people to take action. Washington, DC is home to dozens of monuments etched with beautiful, powerful words from some of our country's greatest leaders. Working in public service, these monuments serve as a reminder of impactful leadership for Dean.

Rhetoric is a significant part of leadership. Leaders must use their words intentionally and be mindful of the impact that language can have on others—both positively and negatively.

Learning to Speak Up

Speaking up when it's not easy is a sign of great leadership, according to Dean. Great leaders emerge from difficult situations when it's easier to ignore what's happening than get involved. Dean learned this behavior from her father who was a strong business leader in the pharmaceutical industry and has modeled this behavior throughout her own life.

Her father believed in the mission of research and development to come up with new therapies, new drugs, and new devices to help people live better lives. He believed in doing what was right and was unafraid of being honest if something was going wrong and spoke up if there were complaints or ill effects. When he died, his longtime employer referred to him as "the conscience of our company."

"He was just unafraid to lead," said Dean. "He couldn't be silent in the face of something that was going wrong."

Our history books are filled with strong leaders who had the courage to speak up in the face of adversity. For example, Bobby Kennedy exhibited fearless and compassionate leadership advocating for the poor and marginalized. "He is a reminder that public servants should act out of love as well as good policy," says Dean. Martin Luther King is another great example of a leader who crafted beautiful, inspiring arguments that made a huge impact on the civil rights movement.

To effectively influence others, a leader must develop and hone their communication skills. It's not just what you say, it's how you say it. Leaders must be mindful of their body language, tone of voice, and choice of words when communicating.

Taking Action

Growing up with strong leadership influences, Dean exhibited leadership potential at an early age. As a teenager, she enjoyed working at a local flower shop and earning a little extra spending money. While the other young workers stood around and talked after they completed a task or assignment, Dean would ask if there was anything else that needed to be done. "I always remember liking my work, loving my work, and taking the lead to want to do more," says Dean.

While people can exhibit leadership qualities from early age, Dean doesn't believe that anyone is born a leader. "Leadership is made through circumstance, compassion, heart, passion, and experience," says Dean. "I think true leaders fail a lot."

Leaders need to leverage failure and use it as a learning opportunity. For Dean, she has learned to find inspiration in her failures. As a freshman in congress, Dean was disappointed that she couldn't make a bigger difference on the issue of gun violence during her time in the statehouse. Despite only being a freshman, she co-founded the PA SAFE Caucus.

Dean was chided by a more senior state legislature member who said that she had no business forming a caucus because she didn't know what she was doing and was out of her depth. Dean did it anyway.

The atmosphere in Harrisburg, PA around the issue of guns and gun violence was so very difficult during her tenure. This no doubt hindered her ability to move the needle very far on the issue. But unwilling to let failure stand in her way,

Dean was encouraged by the words of civil rights leader John Lewis, "Keep your eye on the prize. Do not be down. Do not get discouraged. Keep your eye on the prize."

"I guess I'm hoping to learn from him," says Dean. "If he can have that kind of patience, faith, and optimism that we will make a difference, I can have it too."

Women Leadership Challenges

Dean echoes this sense of optimism and hope for the future of women in leadership. A record number of women are serving in the 116th Congress with women accounting for nearly a quarter of both chambers. She is encouraged by this movement in getting more women into political office.

In just her short time in office, Dean has seen progress. Just a few weeks after being sworn into the House in Harrisburg, she spoke for the first time. There was a payday lending bill that was being considered and being pushed by the payday lending lobby that Dean opposed. She just had an overwhelming feeling consume her that pushed her to speak on the issue. So, she got in queue and spoke on the floor.

While gratifying that she voiced her concern on a topic she felt strongly about, the speaker told her that it was inappropriate that she spoke. He privately told her, "You're a freshman. You should sit, and listen, and learn."

Dean rebuked by saying, "Well, with all respect, Mr. Speaker, I was elected to serve now. My constituents did not say to sit here and be quiet for two years. I was elected to serve." Dean continued to speak up in the Pennsylvania

General Assembly and the Speaker several times more asked her to stop.

So, finally, one day, a person who runs the floor came up to her and said, "You're my hero." With a puzzled look, Dean asked why. He said, "Because you keep speaking up." While the Speaker said that freshmen shouldn't speak, he really meant that freshmen women shouldn't speak.

It was telling of the times, but that climate has since changed. While we're seeing a positive shift in the right direction, there are still many challenges that women must overcome.

"It has been my experience that women are judged by how we speak more than men," says Dean. "While men can yell and pound on tables and still claim a sense of dignity, women are judged as shrill. I guess, in the end, I think you just earn your credibility regardless of gender, one committee meeting at a time, one piece of legislation at a time, one speech on the floor at a time. You earn your credibility, and then I think you are a co-equal. I do believe it's changing, but we'll see."

This optimism for change leaves Dean hopeful for the future. A future where it will no longer be surprising that women hold top positions. A future where leadership is equal. A future that reclaims the ethics of good governance that public service ought to be.

LEADERSHIP LESSON

Based on your experience as a leader and as a follower, what are the challenges that get in the way of speaking up?

Identify three members of your current team:

Assess each team member's level of comfort to speak up and rate them on the following scale: 1—Never speaks up; 3—Intermittently speaks up; 5—Always speaks up.

Member Name 1:

Assessment:

Identify one action you can take to positively impact this individual's comfort level to speak up.

Member Name 2:

Assessment:

Identify one action you can take to positively
impact this individual's comfort level to speak up.

Member Name 3:

Assessment:

Identify one action you can take to positively
impact this individual's comfort level to speak up.

JUSTIN MORGAN

Author Introduction

If it wasn't for change, people would care a whole lot less about leadership.

The first time you sit down with Justin Morgan you can almost immediately sense his innate intelligence. He doesn't flaunt it, or throw it in your face, or go out of his way to place his IQ on center stage in a demeaning way, but the capacity to naturally and effortlessly wrap his head around things that are truly complex then explain them, both practically and conversationally, is readily apparent. As you come to grips with his talent, your mind wanders ever so briefly. You imagine being a friend of his in high school (not so very long ago, by the way). He'd be the guy that would call you up and say:

"Hey ... let's go do fun things!"

And you'd want to, of course, but would wind up saying something like:

"Man, I would love to, but I have to study."

Then he'd probably say something like:

"Oh ... OK ... no problem!"

At which point you would study like crazy (and he wouldn't). Then when the test came around, he would ace it and you would struggle despite your documented sacrifice. Morgan has that kind of frustrating, but equally admirable, intelligence.

But, as we all know at this point, a lot of times people with high IQs struggle with things like emotional intelligence and leadership, right? Not so with Morgan. With every word that comes out of his mouth you feel like you are sitting across from a thirty-year-old Peter Drucker. He is both a student and a seasoned practitioner of influence.

For example, he understands change. He gets it intuitively, intellectually, and operationally. When addressing the topic of leadership, he imbeds his answer in the ongoing waves of change:

> "I have to believe that if it wasn't for change, people would care a whole lot less about leadership. As a matter of fact, the best advice I could offer to a young person that is interested in becoming a better leader is to really lean into change. Because when I started out, I think I just thought that the best ideas would somehow always win. But they don't. And when you unpack that uncomfortable reality a little bit, you recognize it's primarily because not everyone is wired like you are ... and that's really unsettling."

"I think lots of people can create a comparatively desirable vision of the future and even get a good number of people excited about it. But when it comes time to step out on the thin ice and execute against the hypothetical image you have created, it's unsettling, and it's scary, and it sort of shakes you at your core. The only way you can really 'take your temperature' as a leader is to intentionally put yourself into those kinds of circumstances and pay very close attention to how you respond."

And, as we believe the pages that follow will demonstrate, the more you peel the onion back on Morgan's leadership journey, the more evidence you see of a highly motivated and highly successful leader, driving meaningful change in a massive organization that is episodically notorious for complying with bylaws that stand in stark contrast to its overall mission.

"If what we're doing is not helping people live remarkable lives, then let's change what we're doing."

- Justin Morgan

SERVING OTHERS
Justin Morgan

Leadership and Change

Some definitions of leadership fall flat with shallow references to direct eye contact and firm handshakes. The characteristics that embody a true leader have much greater depth. Leadership requires vision, making tough decisions and being responsive and adaptive to other people. Leaders provide direction and inspire purpose. They are curious and passionate about what they're doing, and they play the role of the student as much as the teacher.

Justin Morgan has learned the value that comes from becoming a student of his colleagues, congregation, and his community. Being a leader of a volunteer-run organization like a church comes with its share of challenges and opportunities for growth.

"Leadership really starts by leading yourself," believes Morgan. Leaders must be open to change and continually push themselves to grow and evolve. They must also surround themselves with innovative people and be receptive to new ideas.

When you think about it, "Leadership is the ability to create change," says Morgan. People who can help organizations and individuals leave an impact on the world. While change can be exciting and bring positive results, it can also create uncertainty and fear. Successfully navigating through change is all part of a leader's journey.

The Leadership Journey

In his early 20s, Morgan found himself in a job where change needed to happen, and it was his responsibility to negotiate that change. He was working as a youth director at a church with a congregation of 5,000 members but only had 30 kids attending the youth group.

When Morgan was hired, he was simply told to change that. This was the first time that he was given a problem and asked to find the solution without any specific instructions. It was his responsibility to increase attendance at their youth group. Morgan recalls feeling an overwhelming sense of apprehension.

During this time, Morgan had not yet come to terms with what leadership meant to him. He assumed everyone was just wired the same way and had the same talents and direction. It took him time to realize that people are complex and what motivates one person doesn't necessarily motivate the other.

In his new role, Morgan leaned into his innate gifts of creating vision, clarity, and focus to achieve his goals. As the strategy grew into a more defined plan, Morgan realized that he needed to recruit new talent with fresh ideas to be successful. In other words, he needed to learn how to share the workload.

Up to this point, Morgan had spent little time refining his interpersonal skills or thinking about how to appropriately bring people together and delegate tasks. He jokes that "his job would be easy if it weren't for people." He realizes that this is probably true not only of the church, but for all organizations.

It's the people part that's tough. Entering this next chapter in his leadership journey required a strong focus on relationship management.

"When I started in leadership, I just thought the best ideas win," says Morgan. "I realized pretty quickly that ideas and charisma honestly have a pretty low ceiling and a short expiration date, but that the great leaders out there are committed to their people."

Morgan has learned to ask great questions and devote time to giving his colleagues the floor and listening. "If I'm doing my job right, I'm listening more than I'm speaking," says Morgan. It is through listening that he has learned how to lead more effectively.

Serving Others

Becoming a leader requires a lot of adjustment, especially when it comes to gaining perspective. Leaders must adjust their focus away from their own agenda and success and focus their energy on the success of those around them. It's about helping other people grow and championing their accomplishments.

Reflecting on great leaders in his own community,

Morgan has recognized that these individuals didn't necessarily have the best ideas, but what stands out most is how they have created cultures that were developing people.

Working in a volunteer-based organization, there's definite benefits and drawbacks. It is a different relationship in this type of environment where there isn't a paycheck tied to the service that people provide the church. It is often assumed that you can't fire a volunteer, but Morgan quickly clarifies that it happens quite often.

"Some of the greatest pastors are like great CEOs," says Morgan. "They care so much about their mission, and their vision, and the people who are supporting them that they will make the hard decisions when they have to for the sake of the mission."

Working in a church environment, Morgan has access to a large pool of talent. He is constantly "interviewing" and scanning the room for the next great talent, which he realizes is a huge competitive advantage over other companies. Having this talent pool enables Morgan and his leadership team to bring new perspectives and ideas to the table.

Studying the Competition

Identifying your competition is essential in determining your mission and goals—even for a church. One would assume that a church's competition would be other churches and religions, but Morgan holds a different perspective.

"We wanted to be a part of creating change for the church, which would require us to have different competition," he says. "We weren't really interested in just trying to compete in the existing models of how church happens but wanted to create a new model or innovate in some new ways."

Being located in downtown Raleigh, North Carolina, Morgan and his team turned their attention not to other churches, but toward local coffee shops and restaurants, the morning news channels, the beach and mountains, and just plain rest and relaxation.

Morgan's leadership team wanted to figure out a way to connect with people who weren't connecting with any other faith community. Finding ways to create excitement around attending church in the face of more enticing options is a critical focus area for the team. "How do we create an environment that's as compelling, that provides as much peace, comfort, or inspiration as any of those other places?" questions Morgan. To help solve this problem, Morgan and his team became students of those organizations.

Even with this modern-day mission, they wanted to be honest that they are a church and they do have a certain perspective that they're offering to the world. But they wanted to try to bring it humbly. The church Morgan leads is founded on the principle that we all imitate or follow somebody. From the clothes that we wear to the car that we drive, we make decisions every day that are influenced by other people and organizations.

"Our church recognizes this about people and believes that everyone owes it to themselves to ask the question, 'Who am I following and are they worth imitating?'" says Morgan.

The church believes that Jesus lived a compelling and remarkable life that's worthy of imitation, and so they want to encourage society to reflect on who they're imitating. At the end of the day, Morgan's main mission is for people to leave his church kinder, more forgiving, and gracious.

"If what we're doing is not helping people live remarkable lives, or lives that are worth imitating, then let's change what we're doing," says Morgan.

With a relentless spirit, Morgan is constantly challenging his leadership team to evaluate whether their strategy is working. "If not, let's not go another day down this path and make the adjustments now, and figure out, and experiment, and keep that entrepreneurial spirit alive and not just rest in that," he says.

Morgan chooses to see these moments of reflection as a gift to redirect focus and create a new solution. He views this as getting back to the "sweet spot of where change happens."

Striking a Balance

The challenge for those who are passionate about their work is that they can be so driven and purpose-oriented at work that they check out when it comes to their family life. Leaders can be so focused on developing people at work that this same mission doesn't translate at home to strengthening their own family.

Morgan is constantly challenged to bring all of that same passion, energy, and focus to developing his kids.

He wants to create a shared sense of purpose for his family as he does at work.

"It's kind of a humbling realization that I have pretty regularly that, in the same way that I need to be growing as a leader at work, I need to be growing as a husband and a father regularly at home," Morgan says. "If those two things aren't happening at the same time, pretty soon, that integrity that I want for my life, it will impact both. I can't just be an incredible leader and neglect my family because pretty quickly I won't be that great of a leader. They both have to rise together."

The next chapter for Morgan is learning how to balance home and family and creating the space, time, and intentionality that his family deserves.

Assess and Reassess

The leadership journey is never-ending. There are countless opportunities for growth, reinvention, and innovation. Morgan is almost a decade into his leadership journey and has learned many valuable lessons, two of which stick out to him. One is not to be passive when it comes to initiating change, and the other is the critical role that evaluation plays in your success as a leader and as a person.

"People should not wait for the title of leader to be given to them through formal recognition," encourages Morgan. Everyone can take steps to initiate change. Whether you're a volunteer or staff member at any level, "There's some opportunity for you to initiate change, to begin to lean into the process of leading something," believes Morgan.

"I think one of the traps that a lot of people fall into is that they wait for somebody to give them the title or to give them influence to bestow them with that," he says.

Most of the leaders who Morgan has met throughout his journey created influence, no one handed it to them. He cautions that it's a mistake to wait for somebody to invite you to change something. Sometimes diving in and offering input is the best route to take.

The need for continuous evaluation and self-reflection is another takeaway for Morgan. Examining the entire process and evaluating how that experience went is necessary to achieve and maintain success.

So much of leadership for Morgan has been about the really painful experience of "watching the tape." From listening to his sermons to asking for feedback from his colleagues and congregation, Morgan has realized the path to becoming a better leader lies in that feedback. "It isn't without pain, but it's worth it," he believes.

"Great leaders are always willing to hear other voices," Morgan added. "They're always willing to collaborate and bring people together. They have a healthy ego that lets other people win in front and around them."

It may be one of the most challenging aspects of leadership, but it's the people-part that ultimately defines great leaders. And Morgan has learned that well.

LEADERSHIP LESSON

What can you do as a leader to ensure the best ideas win?

Based on your personal experience, describe the relationship between leadership and change.

As a leader, describe the similarities and differences between influencing your peers (or volunteers) and influencing direct reports.

DARYL DAVIS

Author Introduction

If you don't read another chapter in this book, we'd sincerely suggest you take the time to read this one. Perhaps two or three times. Because if you are anything like us, it may take you a time or two to truly come to grips with the talent and tenacity of Daryl Davis, as well as the jaw-dropping results this gifted pioneer has been able to deliver.

In a world where we are inundated with representatives of opposing views screaming at each other before a moderator cuts to commercial break, Davis is a salmon swimming directly upstream. His approach to influencing people that have lived their lives believing things and behaving in a manner that could best be described as hostile and threatening is to invest, to understand, and to create dissonance. The kind of dissonance that forces the targets of his leadership to rethink the foundation of their hostility, voluntarily surrender their hatred, and transform in a manner they, and those around them, never thought was possible.

There are few people in the world that know more about racism, in general, and the Ku Klux Klan (KKK), in particular, than Davis. It would by no means be a stretch to say that through a series of seemingly random events in his exceedingly unique life, Davis became obsessed with the KKK. He read everything there was to read about them. He conducted hundreds of personal interviews with card-carrying members of the KKK. He attended a number of cross-burning Klan rallies. The fact that Davis is an African American provides additional insight into the conviction that drove the research associated with his calling.

Davis graduated from Howard University with a bachelor's degree in music. He has played professionally in bands his entire life, most notably with Chuck Berry, Jerry Lee Lewis, B.B. King, Muddy Waters, and Bruce Hornsby. He was awarded the Best Traditional Blues/R& B Instrumentalist at the 2009 Washington Area Music Awards. Based on personal experience, if you ever have the opportunity to hear Davis play the piano, take it!

His proficiency as a musician led to a moment of truth in his life that turned out to be the genesis of his adult activism. He was playing a gig with a band whose other members were all white in an all-white club in Frederick, Maryland in 1983. When the band took a break, a patron of the club approached Davis and enquired:

> "Where in the world did a black man learn to play the piano like Jerry Lee Lewis?"

That uninformed inquiry led to a conversation, which led to an exchange of phone numbers, which led to an extended dialogue, that resulted in a series of introductions to an extended cadre of Klansmen, that has resulted in over two hundred members renouncing their allegiance and crediting Davis as the impetus for their departure from the KKK. To date, forty-five of those former Klansmen have ceremoniously contacted Davis, informed him of their decision and the reasons for it, and provided him with their KKK hoods and robes as a symbolic gesture of his impact on their lives.

But the seed for Davis' activism was planted much earlier in his life. He was ten years old and it was 1968. His father was an officer in the Foreign Service, so Davis had lived his early childhood abroad. On this day, he was the flag bearer for his Cub Scout pack in Belmont, Massachusetts during a local parade. Out of nowhere, adults and children began throwing rocks and bottles at him from the sidewalk as they screamed obscenities. The other scouts and leaders from his pack—all white—formed a human shield, of sorts, to protect him. After the incident, he had his first discussion with his parents about racism. He posed a question that has remained the essence of his life's most important work: "How can they hate me ... when they don't even know me?"

"You have to take a leadership role if you're going to try and persuade somebody and set an example that is influential."

– Daryl Davis

INFLUENCING CHANGE THROUGH OPEN COMMUNICATION

Daryl Davis

Ignorance Breeds Fear

Daryl Davis is a blues musician with a very interesting pastime. For the past fifty years, Davis, an African American, has searched for the answer to a question that has plagued him since he was ten years old: "How can you hate me, when you don't even know me?" And he has searched for the answer to this question in the most unlikely place—through candid conversations with members of the Ku Klux Klan (KKK).

Davis has leveraged the power of simple conversation to dig into the psychology behind racism and influence change. Through the course of his research into this topic, two hundred members of the KKK have given up their robes, says Davis, all of which he covers in his acclaimed book, *Klan-Destine Relationships.* As a race relations expert, he delivers passionate lectures at universities, high schools, churches, civic organizations, and corporations all over the world. His approach to race relations forces people to confront their own prejudices and overcome their fears.

"Ignorance breeds fear. Fear breeds hatred. Hatred breeds destruction," says Davis. It's this snowball effect that can set a destructive chain of events into action, and the only way to stop it is through open communication to eliminate the ignorance. Listening with the intent to understand has the unique ability to connect rather than divide.

"I have this theory," says Davis, "that when two enemies are talking, they are not fighting. They're talking. They might be yelling and screaming and beating their fists on the table to make a point, but at least they're talking. It's when the talking ceases, when the conversation ceases, that the ground becomes fertile for violence. So, we want to keep the conversation going. If you spend five minutes with your worst enemy, you will find something in common."

It's this commonality that connects us as humans to help bridge the gap between our differences and create a foundation of understanding.

Revelations

"Telling somebody something and experiencing it are two different things," says Davis. "For example, how do you tell your daughter to go to school, work hard, get straight A's, and get a great job. And then when your daughter does just that, she ends up making less money than a male colleague who does the same job and the same amount of work. How do we prepare people for that potential reality?"

This is just one example of the situations that Davis brings to the forefront in his lectures. How do you prepare people for discrimination before they've even encountered it?

Davis was ten years old the first time he encountered racism. He had never even heard the term "racism" until his parents sat him down to explain why people would throw garbage at him as he carried the American flag in a parade with the other members of his Cub Scout pack. He couldn't fathom why he was the only person being targeted. He thought for sure those people just didn't like the scouts. His parents explained that he was targeted because of the color of his skin, but Davis thought his parents were lying. He couldn't understand why anyone would hate him when they didn't even know him.

> "I couldn't find any rationale between people throwing things at me and my parents telling me it's because of the color of my skin," says Davis. "I didn't believe them. But I get it now."

After graduating from high school, Davis attended Howard University where he earned a music degree. While music became his full-time profession, studying race relations became his obsession. Davis bought every book he could find on black supremacy, white supremacy, anti-Semitism, the Ku Klux Klan, and neo-Nazism to understand how someone would acquire that ideology. And, as he has learned through his years of research, there's nothing rational about racism.

Finding Inspiration through a Chance Meeting

In 1983, country music had made a resurgence due to the hit movie *Urban Cowboy* starring John Travolta. During this time, if you wanted to work as a full-time musician, you needed to join a country band. So, Davis joined a country band as the only black member.

The band frequently played in Frederick, Maryland—which was a stronghold for the Ku Klux Klan. The band would often play at the Silver Dollar Lounge, a predominately white bar. One evening after the band finished its first set, Davis made his way across the dance floor to sit down when a white gentleman came up behind him and put his arm around his shoulder.

The guy said, "Man, I really like y'alls' music." Davis thanked him and shook his hand. The man complimented his piano playing and said, "This is the first time I ever heard a black man play piano like Jerry Lee Lewis."

While this did not offend Davis, he did find it surprising that this man didn't know the origin of Jerry Lee Lewis' style of piano playing and didn't believe that Jerry Lee learned anything from black people. The man offered to buy Davis a drink, which he agreed to, even though he doesn't drink. Davis ordered a cranberry juice, which the man paid for, and clinked Davis' glass to toast him. After this cordial moment, the man shared that this was the first time he had ever sat down and had a drink with a black man. This completely shocked Davis.

Davis was twenty-five years old at the time and had shared thousands of meals, beverages, and conversations with white people up to that point in his life, and this guy, who was probably in his forties, had never sat down with one black man. Davis inquired as to why, but the man just looked at the tabletop and didn't answer. So, Davis asked him again.

The man's friend urged him to tell Davis, and so the man looked back at Davis and said, "I'm a member of the Ku Klux Klan." Davis burst out laughing because he could not believe what he was hearing. Davis had every book written on the KKK and none of them talked about Klansmen embracing a black man, praising him for his talent, and then buying him a drink on top of that. It didn't make sense.

The man handed Davis his KKK membership card as proof. After chatting for a bit longer, the man gave Davis his phone number and asked him to call whenever his band played at the bar so he could bring his friends. Davis agreed and kept his word. The band played at the bar every six weeks and the man would bring other Klan members to the show. This went on until the end of 1983 when Davis quit the band.

After quitting the band, it dawned on Davis that he missed the perfect opportunity to get the answer to the question that he'd been looking for since age ten: "How can you hate me, when you don't even know me?"

Who better to ask than someone who would join an organization that has a history of hating people based on the color of their skin? Davis envisioned traveling the country interviewing different Klan members and compiling those interviews into the first book written by a black author on the Ku Klux Klan. So, he got to work.

Meeting with the Enemy

Roger Kelly, the Grand Dragon for the state of Maryland, was the first person who Davis wanted to interview for his book. To make this connection, Davis reached out to the

Klansman he befriended at the Silver Dollar Lounge in hopes that he would introduce him to this high-ranking Klansman leader. Unable to locate a telephone number for his old friend, Davis found his home address and showed up to his residence unannounced. While his friend was surprised to see Davis, Davis was also surprised to learn that his friend was no longer a member of the KKK.

After listening to how his friend no longer believed in the KKK ideology, Davis shared his book idea and asked his friend to introduce him to Roger Kelly. His friend refused out of the danger of the request. Davis begged and pleaded with him to give him the address and phone number of Mr. Kelly. Finally, after about twenty minutes of begging, he gave it to Davis on the condition that he not reveal to Mr. Kelly where he got his personal information. Davis agreed and his friend warned him not to show up to Kelly's house because he would be killed. His friend explained that there was a Klan bar up in Thurmont, Maryland if he wanted to meet Mr. Kelly. Davis took notes and set out to find Mr. Kelly for his first interview.

Discussing his schedule with his secretary, Mary, Davis selected a Sunday to drive up to Thurmont. Mary, a white woman, asked to go with him. Davis refused due to the riskiness of the situation. He finally gave in and allowed her to come at her own discretion. They made the hour-and-a-half drive to the bar and waited for hours to no avail. The trip was a bust without meeting any Klansmen.

The next day Davis asked Mary to call Roger Kelly to set up an interview for the book. While he could have called

Mr. Kelly himself, Davis felt it would be better if Mary set up the call in case Mr. Kelly was reading into the voice of the individual on the phone and could detect a black voice from a white voice. Mary called and set up an interview at a hotel. Mr. Kelly agreed to the interview.

Roger Kelly showed up to the interview with the Grand Nighthawk, his bodyguard. Wearing camouflage, the bodyguard walked in and scanned the room when he noticed Davis sitting at the table and he froze. Davis introduced himself and shook the Nighthawk's hand. Mr. Kelly took a seat and asked Davis for identification, which Davis obliged.

Mr. Kelly let Davis know right from the start that black people are inferior to white people. Black people have smaller brains than white people. They are prone to criminal activity, laziness, and take advantage of the government welfare system. Basically, every stereotype you can imagine.

Davis wasn't there to fight with Mr. Kelly. He was there to listen and learn from him. Davis came to the meeting with a vast amount of knowledge on the Ku Klux Klan and had a Bible readily available so Mr. Kelly could point to the exact verse whenever he cited the Bible as justification.

The interview proceeded rather uneventfully until there was a loud noise that put everyone on edge. Kelly and Davis locked eyes, and no one said a word. They were silently reading each other. Unbeknownst to them in that moment of tension, the noise was only ice shifting in a metal beverage bucket. It was Mary who made the connection, and everyone burst out laughing.

Davis felt that served as a teaching moment. All due to the ignorance of a foreign noise entering their comfort zone, they became fearful and accusatory of each other. "Ignorance breeds fear," says Davis. "We fear those things we don't understand. If you do not put a cap on that fear, that fear will escalate to hatred because we hate those things that frighten us. If you don't cap that hatred, that will escalate to destruction, because we want to destroy those things that we hate. Why? Because they frighten us. But guess what? They may have been harmless and we were just ignorant."

"If you want to solve this issue," says Davis, "we need to stop addressing the symptoms. We need to stop addressing the hatred, stop addressing the fear. Go to the source. And fix the source. Address the ignorance. If you get rid of the ignorance, then there's nothing to fear. And you fix ignorance with education. You bring enlightenment and you alleviate the ignorance."

Influence and Change

Influence is a core leadership skill. A leader is any person who can influence others whether they hold an executive title at a Fortune 500 company or happen to be a neighbor in the community. As a musician, Davis not only understands the effect that music can have on human emotion, but he also understands that open communication and listening is a pathway to finding common ground and influencing change.

"You have to take a leadership role if you're going to try and persuade somebody and set an example that is influential," says Davis. "We only have one chance to make a good first impression. We may have a second or third chance to make a good impression, but one chance to make a good first impression. When you're trying to cultivate a relationship with someone, it usually takes more than one meeting."

Over countless interviews with members of the Klan, Davis has learned that "whether they like you or not, if they find you to be credible that first time, then chances are they will meet with you again."

Davis has interviewed hundreds of Klan members and attended dozens of Klan rallies over the years. He has discovered that while you are actively learning about someone else in these moments, you are also passively teaching them about you.

Davis views this as an opportunity and obligation to lead by example to influence change. At the end of the day, everyone has something to offer and everyone has something to learn. "We need to give people a platform to express themselves," says Davis. "We don't have to believe their views, but we should be listening."

"When you suppress free speech, it's going to fester and it's going to explode," warns Davis. "You want to let it come out and hear it so you can figure out how to address it."

Finding Answers
Davis has spent decades searching for the answer to his question: "How can you hate me, when you don't even know me?" The answer to that question has changed over time from illogical conclusions about his small brain and

propensity for violence due to the color of his skin to affirmations from members of the Klan who have said, "You know, Daryl, I don't hate you. I can't hate you. I know you. And you're not these things."

The author C.S. Lewis once said, "You can't go back and change the beginning, but you can start where you are and change the ending." Davis echoes this sentiment, believing that children are our greatest resource. It's the ten-year-old children of today who can impact change by providing others with a platform to express themselves and listening with the intent to understand.

LEADERSHIP LESSON

What bias have you struggled with the most during your career?

What is the source of that bias?

What can you do or what have you done to combat or neutralize that bias?

What can you do as a leader to help others recognize and act against their biases?

ANN HERRMANN-NEHDI

Author Introduction

It is difficult to imagine Ann Herrmann-Nehdi in a bad mood. We are confident she has them, of course, but we're betting they don't come around all that often ... or last all that long when they do. As a matter of fact, if you had to lock in on a single word that described her it would have to be energy. The positive kind. The kind that is uncontrollably contagious. The kind you can literally feel in a room when she takes center stage and starts telling whoever is in earshot things like:

- What would it look like if we took action on that problem right now?

- I think it could seriously make a huge difference around here ... how about you?

- Of course, it would be difficult ... but that sort of comes with the territory ... right?

- And even though it would be difficult ... no doubt we could make it fun, too ... right?

- But the main thing is that a year from now we could be looking back on something we did together that made a positive contribution ...

• Who's with me?

If all that seems a little far-fetched, we assure you … it is not. Herrmann-Nehdi has forever been "the straw that keeps stirring the drink." Case in point, years ago, someplace in or around Stamford Connecticut, a young Ann Herrmann was ready to enter the world of commerce. She approached the franchise owner of a popular newspaper on the front porch of his home to ask about a job. That exchange went something like this:

> **Ann:** Mr. Cox, my name is Ann Herrmann and I'd like to talk with you about a job selling newspaper subscriptions.
>
> **Mr. Cox:** I appreciate that young lady, but this is a job for boys.
>
> **Ann:** But that isn't what you really care about, is it?
>
> **Mr. Cox:** It isn't?
>
> **Ann:** No! You care about selling newspaper subscriptions! Why would it matter if a boy sold them or a girl?

And as a small glass ceiling shattered on Mr. Cox's front porch that day, Ann was given an opportunity. To the surprise of absolutely no one that knew her, she made the most of it as well (along with pretty much all the other opportunities that she has talked her way into since!).

Currently, Herrmann-Nehdi is consumed with the ongoing exploration of the brain. Her father, Ned Herrmann, is accurately referred to as "father of Whole Brain®

technology." A graduate of Cornell University who majored in physics and music, Ned had a career of true significance that included heading up management education at General Electric. He spent over thirty years enhancing creative thinking capabilities and making foundational contributions to all things leadership, relationship building, and communications. Any guesses on who was instrumental in assisting with his early research?

We have no idea what you did with your father when you made your way home after school as a kid, but Ann was busy having electrodes strapped to her head to monitor her cerebral tendencies! To take it a step further (a true story that brings to mind images of Robert De Niro and Ben Stiller in *Meet the Parents*), Ned would also monitor the brain patterns of Ann's boyfriend. Can you even imagine?!

The product of all that was a model that has been used around the world for decades to help leaders lead and truly leverage their cognitive diversity (which every organization already has—they just might not know it or measure it!). We would encourage you to check out one of Herrmann-Nehdi's TEDx[1] Talks to garner some insight on how you might wake up your own brain but, in the meantime, please read this chapter. If nothing else, we are convinced you will get some valuable insight into not only how to talk the leadership talk but walk the leadership walk!

---

[1] Herrmann-Nehdi, Ann. "One Thing to Know About Your Brain That Will Change Your Life" and "Think Like Your Future Depends on It, Because It Does." *TEDx Talks*, Jan. 2018, https://bit.ly/326GBnM and https://bit.ly/3mQhcqn.

"The ability to learn
is one of the most
critical skills for
leaders today and
in the future."

- Ann Herrmann-Nehdi

FOSTERING A LEARNING MINDSET

Ann Herrmann-Nehdi

A Lifetime of Curiosity

Learning is often viewed as a childhood activity—something that occurs in the early part of our lives. It's assumed that once we reach adulthood and enter the workforce, learning ends. While we may no longer be attending a formal schoolhouse, learning is a lifelong activity.

The real learning happens in day-to-day life when applying what you learned. "That's where the rubber really hits the road," says Ann Herrmann-Nehdi, chair of the board and chief thought leader of Herrmann Inc. "Those who are not learners are going to really, really suffer and find leadership a real challenge."

Herrmann-Nehdi specializes in the practical application of neuroscience to help leaders improve their impact and more effectively manage change by leveraging their untapped thinking and learning potential. The ability to learn, unlearn, and relearn is critical for today's leaders. With business rapidly changing, leaders who continuously learn and develop are more agile and adaptive to change.

"It's that combination of curiosity, willingness, and interest in learning that allows you to break out of the patterns that might be mentally, from a brain perspective, limiting you in terms of where you might be going," she says.

Humans have the potential to learn and grow over the course of their life. We are not fixed in our thinking or abilities. Leaders must foster a lifelong learning mindset to continuously push themselves to develop their skills to reach their full potential.

Be Self-Aware: Think about your Thinking

Herrmann-Nehdi likes to say, "We become what we think about most," and her personal learning journey is certainly an example. As a leader, Herrmann-Nehdi found herself continuously needing to "drink her own champagne" (i.e., applying Whole Brain Thinking® in her role to enable her to continue to grow). One of her greatest "aha's" came when she learned how to avoid becoming a "prisoner of your preferences." This epiphany came as she was in discussion with a CEO client one day. The client was lamenting how his team seemed to consistently "miss the mark on execution." The reason became very clear: the team's thinking as explained by their HBDI® (Herrmann Brain Dominance Instrument) Profile. The assessment, developed by Herrmann-Nehdi's father, clearly showed a collective low preference for implementation and execution.

The "Four P's" of Whole Brain Thinking®: Profits, Process, People, and Possibilities strongly suggested this team was not attentive enough to elements of process. Coincidentally, that was also Herrmann-Nehdi's least preferred preference!

She suddenly realized why her own executive team was struggling with an operational issue. Her takeaway? Most leaders never stop learning, which means they never stop thinking about their thinking! Herrmann-Nehdi realized she had tools at the ready to help her have the greatest possible impact on her own effectiveness as a learning leader.

Proving Yourself

Stepping into a new role or assuming a new responsibility can create a mixture of emotions—excitement, fear, determination, etc. Ultimately, people want to succeed, especially in the face of resistance. They want to prove that they have what it takes to do the job.

Herrmann-Nehdi exhibited perseverance as a teenager when searching for her first summer job. She heard from a friend that there were open positions selling *New York Times* subscriptions door-to-door. Herrmann-Nehdi applied for the position and was immediately rejected. The franchise owner said, "No, no, no, no. We don't hire girls, it's only guys who do this." His reasoning was based on the weight of the samples she would be required to carry around neighborhoods and didn't believe girls had the endurance or strength to do the job.

After some convincing, she talked the man into giving her a chance. While thrilled to be given the opportunity, Herrmann-Nehdi knew she needed to prove herself—to prove that she could do the job. This pushed Herrmann-Nehdi to develop a completely different approach to selling subscriptions that enabled her to beat all the other guys at their numbers.

While she didn't set out to break through any glass ceilings during this experience, Herrmann-Nehdi does believe there is an uneven burden on women to prove themselves more. This challenge is fueled by misconceptions and unconscious biases that inhibit our thinking. There are still many roadblocks and barriers for women to overcome in order to gain true equality in today's world. Leaders must work to override bias in their own thinking to create more inclusive workplaces.

Proving yourself is not just a challenge for women. "It's tough for anyone to break into something new for the first time," says Herrmann-Nehdi. "It takes perseverance and a willingness to be uncomfortable in the unknown."

Finding Comfort in the Unknown

Many people associate vulnerability with weakness, but it's quite the opposite. It takes strength, confidence, and a level of fearlessness to be vulnerable with others, especially to your team. Leaders who have the courage to be vulnerable can foster higher levels of engagement, trust, and creativity. Instead of avoiding discomfort, these leaders embrace moments of vulnerability by taking responsibility for their actions and asking for help when they need it. Being vulnerable allows leaders to form more genuine connections and create a safe, collaborative environment.

Discomfort can be scary but it's also a sign of growth. Years ago, Herrmann-Nehdi was extremely frustrated with a leadership challenge at work and called a mentor to discuss the situation. As the mentor listened to her talk, he remained quiet and then said, "I am so excited to hear how frustrated you are." This was not the feedback she was expecting to hear. He went on to say, "Yeah, because discomfort is a sign of learning."

"That shift of mindset is essential for leaders," says Herrmann-Nehdi. "You've got to be able to step into that zone of discomfort. That is a sign of learning but so many people don't like stepping into it and they certainly don't want other people to see them stepping into it." Herrmann-Nehdi's mentor helped her stretch her thinking by reframing discomfort as an advantage: "Your comfort zone can be your danger zone unless you continuously step outside to stretch."

The most effective leaders can admit when they don't have the answers. Instead of viewing themselves as incompetent or a failure, they choose to use these moments of uncertainty as learning opportunities. They leverage the expertise of their colleagues and peers to formulate a solution and they recognize those contributions in a meaningful way.

Being vulnerable humanizes leaders. It allows employees to see their leader as a person who is faced with challenges and learns from failure. Someone they can relate to. Someone they can respect. "Leaders must be willing to step out of their comfort zone and stretch their thinking," says Herrmann-Nehdi. "That takes energy, motivation, and a willingness to be uncomfortable." Leaders must continually push themselves to learn and grow and find a way to be comfortable with the unknown.

Creating a Learning Culture

Leadership is not a skill that you gain from reading a handful of books or attending a few training courses. "You build your brain over the course of your life through your experiences and the way you engage with people," says Herrmann-Nehdi. "And I think that's how leadership gets built as well." It's a journey of collecting small insights over time that shapes your perspective. Organizations need to recognize that leadership is a continuous process and must promote ongoing learning opportunities.

"And it's not just leadership development," says Herrmann-Nehdi. "Learning needs to be built into our day-to-day work lives in ways that it's not today." It needs to be integrated into the flow of work and not just a separate workshop. Organizations need to build a culture that prioritizes learning and development and cultivates growth.

"Many organizations are failing to cultivate growth in a way that allows everyone to participate," says Herrmann-Nehdi. This is seen in many high-potential talent programs, where employees are assessed and identified based on their potential to succeed in more senior roles in the organization. But, all too often, those types of programs are flawed with bias.

The talent selected for high-potential programs is often a reflection of the leader who selected them. Research supports this theory. When you look at the different thinking preferences—analytical, practical, relational, or experimental—you're going to pick someone who reflects your own preferences, says Herrmann-Nehdi.

To break out of this model, organizations need to create an inclusive culture that brings a variety of perspectives to the table. Leaders must pay attention to their thought process to begin deliberately and consciously overriding their thinking bias(es). "Whether it's something as simple as somebody's thinking style or it's something as profound as racial bias, you've got to be very, very aware. It's not something a lot of people feel comfortable doing today."

Bringing a diverse set of perspectives together to make decisions and solve business problems leads to better outcomes. "Great leaders understand the value of different perspectives—what we call cognitive diversity," says Herrmann-Nehdi, "and they know how to lead through it."

An innovative culture allows people to fail forward. "If you're not taking enough risks, if you're not making enough mistakes, that means you're not trying enough," says Herrmann-Nehdi. Employees need to feel safe to fail. Not in a physical sense but in an emotional sense. They need to feel safe taking risks without fear of retribution. They need to be empowered to make decisions and take chances.

This safe, nurturing culture will allow employee engagement to flourish. It will untap the creative potential of employees and encourage learning and development. "Creating that culture where you're invited, it's safe, you're encouraged, and you have access to growth opportunities that will engage people's brains," says Herrmann-Nehdi. "Leaders and managers have a huge role to play there."

Growth and Opportunity

Leadership is a reflection of personal growth. "Understanding of self is always going to be at the heart of leadership," says Herrmann-Nehdi. Great leaders are students of their craft and continuously strive to learn and grow. "The ability to learn is one of the most critical skills for leaders today and in the future," she says.

The most successful leaders never stop learning—in fact, they model what a learning mindset is. They understand how they and others think and learn—and use that knowledge to create a culture that values difference and encourages people to continuously develop. To foster this learning mindset, organizations need to provide leaders with practical, accessible tools and methodologies that they can use to advance their growth and potential. As business continues to evolve, Herrmann-Nehdi believes there is going to be increased pressure on all employees to become truly activated lifelong learners—not just leaders. This will lead to the creation of more company cultures where learning while working is not only encouraged, it's expected.

LEADERSHIP LESSON

Based on your own experience, what is the relationship between learning, thinking, and leadership?

What is your greatest blind spot as a leader?

☐ Profits   ☐ People
☐ Process   ☐ Possibilities

What value do the following thinking styles from the Whole Brain Model® bring to a team?

- Analytical
- Practical
- Relational
- Experimental

What can you do as a leader to ensure your team has a healthy mix of each—ensuring your blind spot is mitigated?

BRETT WILLIAMS

Author Introduction

When you meet Brett Williams for the first time, you shake the hand of a personable, humble, American hero. He's the kind of guy that has figured out a way to exude confidence without projecting a hint of arrogance. In the for-what-it's-worth category, Williams is a club champion, scratch golfer that genuinely and consistently compliments any decent shot one of his playing partners manages to hit. That makes the fact that he is probably beating you by ten strokes or more a little easier to swallow somehow!

When you find out he was an F-15 pilot in the Air Force for twenty-eight years, you quietly start doing math in your head (he has to be sixty but he looks like he's thirty-something. What's up with that?). When you get to know him a little better, you figure out his secret, or at least one of them: discipline. He's the kind of guy that is up early, probably every single day. He has goals, every day, and he relentlessly pursues them. Even in his post-military career, which should never be confused with "retirement," Williams is the walking, talking embodiment of an "execution animal."

As is the case with many other notable leaders from a variety of different fields, there is nothing overly complicated about his journey. As a young pilot, he watched and he listened. As a result, he became acutely aware of the tenured pilots in his squadron that everybody wanted to fly with. The reputations of those pilots were undeniable and readily on display. Intuitively, Williams started to observe and study those pilots with ever-increasing dedication. What characteristics, traits, and behaviors did those pilots display? How did they build their reputations? What distinguished them from other highly talented peers?

Williams spent time with those leaders every chance he got. He asked them questions. He took notes. He actively sought their input on decisions he needed to make, as well as their feedback on actions he had taken (What could have gone better? What did I miss? What could I have done differently?). Slowly, steadily he molded himself into the kind of leader that personified the characteristics of the leaders he held in high regard during his career. Ultimately, he progressed to the point where he commanded the largest combat wing in the U.S. Air Force (the 18th Wing in Okinawa, Japan). In that capacity, he had operational responsibility for over 9,000 active airmen and served as the de facto mayor, chief of police, etc. for over 25,000 people that lived on the base.

After twenty-eight years, Williams transitioned into the field of IT and cybersecurity. Initially, he was responsible for chief information officer and chief information security officer functions for command and control networks in the Pacific. In his final active duty assignment, Williams served as the director of operations for the United States Cyber Command. Among many other things, he is credited with designing the structure and operational model the Department of Defense continues to follow to protect our national interests from cyber threats.

He was greeted in the cyber community as you might suspect. (No offense, of course, but what qualifications does an F-15 pilot have to lead a cadre of 400 technology specialists waging a war of their own against cyberterrorism?) Technically, the short answer to that question at the time was, "Not many!" But, from the vantage point of leadership and effective influence, Williams had been preparing for this role his entire career. He had no idea going in that his final command in the Air Force would provide him with a springboard to impact hundreds of organizations and tens of thousands of people across industries who are in the midst of fighting their own concentrated battles against cyber risk.

The essence of his lifelong leadership-related study, in combination with his practical leadership experience, confirms that leadership is, indeed, "vague" and that leaders will forever be judged on how well they embrace that ambiguity and effectively manage risk under pressure.

"We all get more done if we don't worry about who gets the credit."

— Brett Williams

LEADERSHIP IS VAGUE

Brett Williams

Leadership Alignment

There is no one-size-fits-all leadership approach. Every leader is unique and must develop a style that works for them. This exploration to become a successful leader starts with the simple act of observation. By observing successful leaders and reflecting on the attributes you admire, new leaders can begin to shape a leadership style that works for them.

Brett Williams, the chief operating officer of IronNet cybersecurity and a retired major general in the U.S. Air Force, has learned firsthand that leadership behavior sets organizational culture. Developing a core set of values and modeling those attributes are critical to consistent and authentic leadership.

"The reputation you have as a leader is not going to be built on what you say," says Williams. "It's going to be built on the observations that people have of you when you're not really paying attention."

Therefore, the words and actions of a leader must align to truly be successful. Leaders must exemplify their values and build a culture based on mutual trust and alignment around a shared vision.

Leadership Agility

After twenty-eight years of working his way up through various levels of operational command in the Air Force, Williams received a call to join the IT and communications community as the director of communication services at U.S. Pacific Command. While his computer science degree from Duke University provided him some basis for the technical aspects of the job, it was his first leadership role in a field not directly tied to aircraft operations.

Transitioning from being a wing commander to leading a technical team was a learning experience. Becoming a new leader, in a new environment, with a new team presented many challenges, but Williams quickly discovered that leadership is "technology agnostic." The fundamental skills and knowledge he gained from his military experience could be adapted to any leadership position, regardless of industry. The principles of empathy and trust are the foundation of successful leadership.

Empathy, Understanding, and Trust

When stepping into any leadership position, leaders must prove their value to the organization and earn the trust of their subordinates, peers, and senior leadership. Trust is never given; it is earned every day. And it can be destroyed in a matter of moments.

Building trust as a leader starts with understanding the people you serve and leveraging that empathy to create a shared vision. Leadership is multidirectional. It can be a top-down function or peer-to-peer with no legitimate power or authority over others.

"Legitimate power is not sufficient," believes Williams. "There's plenty of people who have had legitimate power positions and have not been successful." Communication, building trust, and listening are essential to influencing others, regardless of position.

Employees need to see that leaders listen, consider new ideas, and make changes. Taking a cue from leadership expert Marshall Goldsmith, Williams has learned to "never discount the possibility that somebody else has a good idea." As a leader, you must be present and get down in the layers of the organization and check in with employees. Leaders should ask probing questions to understand how things are going and make sure employees have the resources they need to be successful. Getting that type of feedback opens the communication lines and enables transparency.

Trusting your employees and allowing them to create their own path to a predetermined solution will allow them to feel a sense of ownership over their work. If employees are clear on the vision and objectives, how they get there is irrelevant. The importance is the destination.

Psychological Safety

Leaders must strive to create an environment where people feel safe to offer new ideas, voice concerns, provide constructive feedback, and take risks. Williams has witnessed the impact of this type of leadership in the military and in the private sector.

"When you're sitting at the head of the table and you have eight of your senior folks around there and nobody's asking any questions, nobody's giving you any pushback, everybody's just nodding north and south, something's probably not quite right with the environment that you have set," says Williams.

Psychological safety, the belief that you won't be punished when you make a mistake, is a determining factor of a high-performing team. This type of environment is built on trust and can lead to innovative ideas and breakthroughs. If employees are too afraid to voice their concerns or ideas, then the performance of the team will ultimately suffer.

And so, "It's up to you as the leader to create the environment," says Williams, "especially with those six or seven that you do influence." This is especially critical in large organizations where it becomes necessary for influence to cascade across the business.

At the end of the day, "We play for the name on the front of the jersey, not the name on the back of the jersey," says Williams, drawing inspiration from the legendary Coach Mike Krzyzewski. "If you don't have alignment down there," says Williams, "then you're going have some serious problems." And that alignment starts at the top.

Lifelong Learning
Learning should not end once you become a leader. There are new skills to master and new knowledge to gain, especially if you're a leader in a new field.

"If I don't learn a couple of levels down what's going on," says Williams, "I don't know what the red flags are. And you can't afford to do that."

If you are in a support function and not used to speaking in business terms, then leaders must be accountable for learning the language of business. Leaders must be knowledgeable enough to know when an issue arises and when to start asking questions to find a solution.

"Leaders must also be able to connect the dots for people. Even if you're handing out towels in the gym at an Air Force base in Saudi Arabia, leaders need to communicate how that contributes to airplanes taking off and "putting warheads on foreheads," says Williams.

Connecting those dots instills passion and motivation in employees. If people understand how they're contributing toward the goal, then they are more willing to go above and beyond.

Smart Decision-Making

Successful leaders "make good decisions on less than perfect information," believes Williams. And that skill will become more important as you move up the leadership ladder into more senior positions. This requires a little bit of risk-taking to act before asking for permission.

Working in a safe environment that supports risk-taking can create innovative leaders fueled by passion. However, if you end up in your boss's office begging forgiveness three times a week, then Williams recommends asking for permission a little more often.

Being a smart decision-maker requires getting all the necessary inputs: having a constructive conversation with the right people and executing on the solution. As a leader, it's sometimes difficult to sign off on ideas that were not your own, but, "You can't agonize over the fact that you're not the decision-maker," says Williams.

As a senior leader, "I don't expect you to just blindly go out and do what I want you to do," he notes. Leaders must push back and offer their opinions during discussions. Passively sitting back will only create further discord and misalignment.

At the end of the day, Williams believes that, "We all get more done if we don't worry about who gets the credit." It's this type of environment that embraces new ideas and supports risk-taking. Business is all about managing risk and allocating resources to mitigate and reduce risk. Creating a safe organizational culture that thrives on positive conflict can lead to long-term success.

LEADERSHIP LESSON

What are two things you can do as a leader to improve your level of clarity on an impending decision or course of action?

Consider the statement below and rate it on the following scale: 1—High fear; 3—Unsure; 5—High trust.

How would you rate the psychological safety of those in your command?

What can you do as a leader to improve the psychological safety of those in your command?

JIM DUNCAN

Author Introduction

There are certain people in life that can walk into a room and no matter where that room happens to be or who might be in it at the time, they command attention. By any objective standard imaginable, Jim Duncan is that kind of person.

A product of the Bronx (which he will proudly make clear to anyone, anywhere, and at any time), Duncan embodies a long and well-documented list of traits and habits frequently attributed to leaders. He works hard. He thrives on competition. He leverages a quick-witted sense of humor to disarm petty conflict. He is grounded by a sense of purpose that allows him to transcend any setback that is the product of any transaction.

He effectively leveraged those mannerisms to marry well over his head. Over the years he has developed and refined an approach to life that allows him to almost seamlessly calibrate his work-related aspirations with his dedicated focus to being the best:

- husband he can be (to his wife Betsy).
- father he can be (to his daughter Kirsten).
- brother he can be (to his siblings Diane and Rick).

- friend he can be (to a wide range of people from seemingly every demographic imaginable).

He regularly speaks of his father with profound respect and admiration. As you will discover in the pages that follow, Duncan's father, Nardin, was a decorated World War II veteran and a legendary NYC police officer. There were many life lessons imparted by the senior Duncan that played a role in molding Jim into the leader he became, but probably none was more important than "following through on the promises you make to others." Without question, that has something to do with the reason Duncan travels back to New York two or three times a month to visit his sister. And we will readily allow for the fact that, at face value, keeping your sister up to speed on the recent events of your life on a regular basis might not seem like such a big deal, until you find out that was something his father asked Duncan to do shortly before he passed and that his sister has been in a coma for over twenty-seven years.

There's something somewhat odd about Duncan's contribution to this manuscript. You would probably be drawn to him as a leader because he talks so much, and so well, but this is a chapter about listening. Then it hits you! The real reason Duncan's words frequently resonate with those he is attempting to influence is because he has invested whatever time was necessary to fully understand and appreciate where they are coming from long before he ever opens his mouth to speak.

Perhaps this is a skill set he developed over the years as a distinguished sales professional and commercial executive;

perhaps it is an innate talent he was born with and has leveraged his entire life in one way or another; or perhaps it is some combination of the two. One thing is for certain, from Duncan's perspective, if you want to effectively lead people, you need to learn how to listen first!

"If you're open to it, you can see leadership in almost every moment of your life."

- Jim Duncan

THE POWER
OF LISTENING

Jim Duncan

Investing in Listening

Listening is a fundamental component of effective communication. Listening skills are necessary to share and express ideas, give appropriate feedback, make sense of information, validate fears and beliefs, and continue an open dialogue with others. Without listening, a true exchange of information cannot take place.

Through years of leadership experience as a successful businessman and politician, Jim Duncan understands the power of listening and the impact it can have on people. When pinpointing effective leaders in our own lives, Duncan maintains that we often circle back to the people who listened to us. It's the people who invest the time to listen to us that tend to be the most influential people in our lives. They are the people we learn leadership from.

In its simplest form, Duncan believes that "leadership has to do with listening and the ability to listen and allowing someone else to speak."

And as Duncan has learned, this simple sentiment is anything but simple to execute. Listening is a process that requires a commitment to another person—a daily investment in helping others feel valued and heard. Effective leaders allow individuals to succeed by giving them a path to take their talents and letting them grow.

Being a leader is both the greatest opportunity and the greatest responsibility we will ever have, Duncan believes. Leaders must take the opportunity to listen to the people who report to them, but the responsibility is in serving—not looking in but looking out and embracing people who want to help you build something.

Leadership in the Ballpark

Leadership emerges at all ages and stages in life. Even young children in the schoolyard can exhibit and spot leadership qualities. Growing up in the Bronx, Duncan recalls a defining moment of leadership during an informal game of stickball.

In typical childhood fashion, captains were identified and team selection ensued. As a child, nobody ever wanted to be the last one chosen. It was a gut-wrenching moment when it was down to you and one other person, with increasing anxiety over whether you would, in fact, be the last one picked.

On this specific day, Duncan remembers the last-round selection, when the kid who was not the best athlete in the neighborhood was the last one chosen. After this boy's name was called, solidifying that he was indeed the last pick, something happened that Duncan would always remember. The team captain who selected this boy walked over, put his arm around him and said, "Hey, we really need you in order to win today."

This encounter has stuck with Duncan through the years. While that team ended up losing the game, this was a sign of leadership at the age of eleven. In that moment, the captain managed to show that he cared and allowed that person to feel valued and an important part of the team.

The ability to instill confidence in another person is a symbol of great leadership at any age. This display of sportsmanship and leadership had a positive, long-lasting effect on not only the child who was chosen last that day but also on the bystanders watching this exchange take place, including Duncan.

Dedication at All Costs

Our most influential role models are often our parents or primary caretakers. Serving in the U.S. Navy during World War II, Duncan's father Nardin (aka Dunc) was a decorated sailor and fought several battles, including the invasion of North Africa, which resulted in the sinking of his ship and killing of half the sailors on board. But Duncan rarely heard war stories from his father. This was a generation of "silent" leaders, who were raised to keep their heads down, work hard, and provide for their families.

After serving in the military, Duncan's father set his sights on serving his community and became a New York City policeman. His father may not have earned a lot of money, but what he lacked in financial security, he made up for in confidence.

"His level of confidence, his ability to allow others, his children in particular, to raise the bar and move on was something that you can't teach," said Duncan. "It was inherent in him based on his life experiences."

Duncan recalled a specific incident in the 1960s during the civil rights riots in the inner city. His father and his partner, who were both white police officers, had arrested an African American who fit the description of a crime suspect. They soon realized that they made a mistake and arrested the wrong man. Despite this discovery, the man remained in jail.

Duncan's father and partner spent the next year looking for the real culprit. They endlessly worked on the case during off-duty hours and even passed up going on vacation that year to find the suspect.

It was this dedication and passion to find the assailant that led to his arrest. After the case was solved, Duncan's father was on the front page of all the newspapers and appeared on *The Merv Griffin Show* as a result. But this newfound fame didn't affect his father. He felt that he was simply doing his job—end of story.

Earning the Right to Play the Game

Being a successful leader starts with the basics—communication, listening, and problem-solving skills. These same skills are essential for being a successful salesman. The ability to perform extensive research on the customer, actively listen to their challenges, and position your product as the solution are necessary to close deals.

After college graduation Duncan had several entry-level sales jobs before accepting a sales position in the emerging high-tech industry at Comdisco, a computer leasing firm. It was at Comdisco that Duncan learned the value of cultivating customer relationships.

During this time in the high-tech industry, computers were not readily available, and customers were slow to make decisions. This required salespeople to exercise patience and learn as much about their clients as possible—including their children's names and hobbies.

"And that's not done overnight," says Duncan. "It's done by listening, showing up, being there, coming in when you know there isn't a transaction for you, and knowing the customer very, very well."

It may have taken years of planting seeds and cultivating the relationship before a deal moved forward. But when it did, the salesperson knew exactly how to position the company's products as the solution the customer needed. They didn't just close the deal; they earned the right to help the customer solve their problem.

"It was not only about earning the right to play the game, it was about earning the right to be in the game," Duncan explained. It was waiting to be invited in as someone that the customer could count on to drive a solution. All of this is achieved through an ongoing commitment to the customer—by putting them first and listening to their needs.

Letting Knowledge Flow from the Bottom-Up

Many organizations operate with a top-down management structure where information is disseminated from senior executives and trickles down to lower-level employees. Senior leaders are often viewed as those with the knowledge, and employees simply execute on the vision of the executive team. But not at Comdisco.

The founder and CEO, Ken Pontikes, frequently stepped out of his office and talked to the sales team—who cultivated the relationships with clients and potential customers. He turned to the salespeople for insight and information.

The sales philosophy at Comdisco was to build something. This mission was fueled by Pontikes' curiosity, frequently asking the salespeople, "What are you building? Where will the client be five years from now?"

When confronted with these questions, Duncan always thought he was being tested. But he wasn't. In fact, it was quite the opposite. Pontikes trusted him and was asking him these questions to gain knowledge. And that's how he managed the company. He made decisions based on the knowledge that he received from his employees. And that's how he trusted where the market was heading—from the information he gained from his trusted employees.

Pontikes built his company from an initial investment of $5 thousand to annual sales of $4 billion by allowing knowledge to flow up to him so that he could effectively lead. For Duncan, it was Pontikes who set the example that leadership starts from the bottom-up. A leader must allow employees to do what they do best and trust the insight and direction that they provide so that the leader can successfully lead.

Learning to Lead

Becoming a first-time manager is an unnerving moment for every leader—even more so when training is not widely available. Decades ago, formalized leadership training was not as prevalent in organizations as it is today. Employees largely learned through trial and error.

Duncan held the position as a high-performing salesman at Comdisco. Garnering recognition from *Forbes* magazine, Duncan was heralded as one of "America's best salesmen." With the company growing rapidly, Duncan made the transition to management.

When he became a first-time manager, Duncan's first instinct was to duplicate himself. He knew firsthand what it took to be a great salesman and he wanted to help other salespeople achieve that same level of success. But, in the process of attempting to create cookie-cutter molds of himself, he learned it was an impossible feat. People are just too different.

Everyone is unique—with varying personalities, abilities, and temperaments. Duncan knew he needed to take a step back and allow others to excel in their own way—without restrictions.

Through lots of trial and error, Duncan learned that "leadership is about allowing others to achieve what they're meant to be—their uniqueness of who they are as individuals." It's about those moments when you're sitting in a meeting and that person who doesn't usually raise their hand, does. Leadership is about giving them the opportunity to say something and, in turn, shocking everyone on the team because no one expected that from that person.

"Everyone has the capacity to be a leader in a given situation," advocates Duncan. But leadership needs to be allowed to blossom. It is through experience and an attention to learning through others that leaders can grow and influence change.

Turning Feedback into Action

As Comdisco rapidly grew from a startup to a billion-dollar company, Duncan learned a valuable lesson—not only in managing people, but in life. To respond to the rapid expansion, the sales department moved toward a "less-is-more" business model. Salespeople would essentially be given fewer accounts to manage with the intent that they could dedicate increased effort and cultivate increased revenue.

In the process, the company merged its two major sales divisions into the same facility to share information more easily on the same accounts. This transition was incredibly difficult, especially on the sales team, and a learning moment for Duncan.

One day a group of account managers on Duncan's team asked him to go out for a beer. Being that they were both colleagues and friends, he agreed. During this outing, the conversation turned toward the topic of work. The employees said, "The one thing that you've taught us all is to listen." Duncan responded by saying, "Oh, yeah. That's the key to selling." And they said, "You're not listening."

It was in this moment that it occurred to Duncan that he just assumed everybody was on board with the merging of the divisions and everyone understood exactly what it was that the company wanted to accomplish.

Armed with this information, Duncan took the feedback from his colleagues and brought in a consultant who watched his leadership style and provided recommendations on improving his management approach. Through various exercises and meetings with the consultants, Duncan was finally able to see that he needed to check his ego and be present in the moment when listening to others. Duncan realized that it was common for him to reach a point in a conversation where he felt that he answered all the questions and assumed the conversation was over. In his eyes, the conversation was over, regardless if the person was still standing in front of him.

This was an eye-opening moment for Duncan to reassess how he got to that point. Leaders need to be open to constructive criticism and feedback, especially from those who genuinely care about you and want you to be successful. By accepting the criticism and using it as motivation to improve, Duncan took his first step toward truly becoming a leader.

Changing Directions

After decades in the sales industry, Duncan retired and turned his attention toward politics. As an American citizen, he didn't like the direction our country was moving in, so he felt compelled to do something about it. He reflected on the example that his father set as a member of the military and as a family man. He wanted to exemplify his father's efforts in passing on a country where opportunity is something that you grab hold of. And if you're willing to work hard, you're going to be successful and happy.

Looking around his community, he was seeing a lot of unhappy people, so he started to volunteer. He always thought politics was left for politicians, but it's really left for the citizens of the country. That's how Duncan viewed it. It's up to the citizens to support the direction of the country.

In the world of politics, Duncan quickly learned that people are set in their ways. When running for a political office, you're encouraged to fit into a mold. There's a prescriptive formula to being the perfect candidate, with lots of advisors telling you what to say and how to act. But that didn't work for Duncan.

He reflected on his days at Comdisco and did exactly what he did at that company: He listened to the people. Duncan set out to build relationships with his voters by attending town hall meetings where he was able to hear the challenges and concerns of the voters directly from them.

While this approach ended up falling in line with what the advisors were encouraging him to do, he had the words of the people who were going to vote for him, not the words of consultants. And that's what was most important to him.

Work-Life Balance

Aside from being a successful businessman and politician, Duncan places a great deal of importance on his personal life. Duncan lives his life by the philosophy that "if your life is your business, you're no good to your business." Duncan maintains that there needs to be an effort to leave work at work so that you can be present at home. As a reminder to keep business separate from family, there was a tree in Duncan's front yard that he called his "worry tree." Once he pulled in the driveway and passed the tree, he wouldn't speak about business anymore. It was time for family. It was time to actively listen to their day and allow them to feel valued and heard.

This separation is important to successful leaders. A person doesn't have to be a leader all the time. It takes a well-rounded person to be a leader. In fact, Duncan warns that you better be a whole person if you're going to be a successful person. Because if you're not, the success is going to end.

Day-to-Day Leaders

There are moments of leadership all around us—in both our business and personal lives. Whether it's watching a mother who is struggling to console her child and stepping in to provide assistance, opening a door for a stranger, or allowing an employee the opportunity to provide input during an important meeting, leadership can emerge in the most average situation. It's that humbleness and willingness to help that people notice and remember. It's allowing someone else to grow as an individual. It's stepping back and listening. You can see leadership in almost every moment of your life if you're open to it.

LEADERSHIP LESSON

Having a worry tree that separates your personal life from your professional life is a good idea. Agree or disagree? Explain your rationale.

Consider the statement below and rate it on the following scale: 1—Highly ineffective; 3—OK; 5—Highly effective.

How effective are you at truly listening to others?

In specific terms, how can you become a better listener?

CLARISSA ETTER-SMITH

Author Introduction

Brené Brown has taught countless people a great number of things in a relatively short period of time. Her lessons are generally grouped under the umbrella of courage but provide value independently as well. Take the whole notion of a rumble. In its purest form, a rumble is a genuine, heartfelt, but almost invariably difficult, conversation. The kind of conversation that many of us, for any number of reasons, lack the intestinal fortitude to initiate.

We think Brené Brown would be very proud of Clarissa Etter-Smith! As a matter of fact, the first word many of her colleagues use to describe her as a leader is "courageous." For example, we have all been in meetings discussing controversial topics with powerful people who lean across a table and ask us some version of this question: What do you think?

Instead of answering from the heart, many of us do a quick check-in with our heads. As the fight-or-flight part of our brain quickly goes into overdrive, we try to read the tea leaves and determine the response that might do us some good but, at a minimum, will do us no harm. By comparison, Etter-Smith is the kind of person who sits in that meeting, looks people straight in the eyes, and calmly articulates a perspective that needs to be heard, but could easily be avoided.

Case in point. Years ago, Etter-Smith worked for a company that had decided to terminate a high-performing and well-respected employee for compelling reasons. The employee said something he should not have said (admittedly) with no malice of forethought. He made a mistake. The press publicized the incident and, in so doing, escalated its visibility. The company responded by severing ties with the employee.

In the aftermath, Etter-Smith was in a room with the people in power and was asked what she thought. While others sat by in silent approval, Etter-Smith walked out on the ledge and answered the question. With nothing to gain and comparatively much to lose, she offered a viewpoint that was anything but well received by the executives in attendance. The company had managed the moment by sacrificing a dedicated employee, who also happened to be a devoted husband and father, because he made a mistake. While consequences for his actions were no doubt in order, the severity of those consequences sent a disturbing message that was heard loud, clear, and companywide. These kinds of rumbles were common for Etter-Smith and people admired her for them.

Other terms used to describe Etter-Smith were *compassion* and *care*. She has always been the kind of person that was not only aware of those who have less but has consistently behaved in a manner that tangibly acted upon that awareness. A colleague of hers from years gone by recounted a story where Etter-Smith had worked extremely hard and achieved results of significance. She was rewarded with a well-earned bonus that she was ecstatic about, because it would allow her to purchase a new roof for her parents at her childhood home back in Kentucky.

In Etter-Smith's case that's not the exception but the rule! She helps people, all the time, with no expectation of being called out for her generosity or celebrated for her efforts. She routinely helps people that need help! So simple it seems unremarkable when, in reality, it is anything but!

"People fail themselves by trying to be what other people want them to be."

- Clarissa Etter-Smith

BEING TRUE
TO YOURSELF

Clarissa Etter-Smith

Leaders Are Instinctive

Leadership is hard to define. It's personal and means different things to different people. A quick internet search of the term will return thousands of unique definitions. While hard to articulate, most people instinctively know when they're in the presence of great leadership.

"People want leadership to be easy to define," says Clarissa Etter-Smith, currently an executive director. "It's not easy to define and it shouldn't be. There needs to be diversity in what leadership looks like for people to be successful at it."

Leaders shouldn't fixate on one specific leadership model. They should follow their natural instincts to cultivate their leadership skills. "You need to be true to yourself," says Etter-Smith. "Sometimes, people fail themselves by trying to be what other people want them to be."

There is a myriad of ways to be an effective leader, and it has nothing to do with position or power. Leaders can exhibit a wide range of characteristics and values, but great leadership is hinged on a leader's ability to influence others to achieve a common goal.

Influence and Leadership

Etter-Smith understands the power of influence. As a high school student, she organized a walkout to protest the administration pushing back the graduation date due to a previous snowstorm. The students felt that they shouldn't be punished for the bad weather and should graduate on time—not a month later. In a matter of hours, Etter-Smith organized a massive walkout of the entire senior class.

It was in that moment that Etter-Smith realized that she held some influence with her classmates and could communicate and inspire them toward a common goal— something they didn't think was possible. That defining moment of keeping people focused on a shared goal has surfaced throughout her professional life.

"One of the biggest challenges for leaders is to keep people focused on things that matter during difficult times," says Etter-Smith. Maintaining a high-performing team that succeeds during tumultuous change within the organization is a challenge for even the best leaders. Staying focused on the things that matter requires leaders to understand their employees.

"You have to see the whole person and especially when an organization is going through a difficult time that could result in people losing their jobs," Etter-Smith says. "If you know your people, and not just what motivates them in the context of doing their job but what motivates them in terms of them living their lives, it's a lot easier to manage through those kinds of situations because you see the person as a whole person."

This level of support and understanding goes a long way with employees. "They know that you are going to support them no matter what happens at the end," she says. "That allows them to focus because they know that, regardless of whether or not they end up being negatively impacted, they're going to have your support no matter what."

Cultivating Leadership

In order to be effective, a leader must continuously strengthen their skills or "flex their muscles," as Etter-Smith puts it. People have natural instincts that, if cultivated, can transform into superior leadership ability. If they're not cultivated, then those skills may never get used.

"It's like muscles that don't get exercised," says Etter-Smith. Leaders need encouragement to exercise those muscles and build those skills from managers, coaches, or colleagues. Specifically, she believes intellectual curiosity and communication are two critical skills for effective leadership.

Great leaders never stop learning. They strive to continuously grow and develop their skills. Etter-Smith uses a unique line of questioning during her hiring process to spot lifelong learners. By asking questions as simple as, "Tell me about the last book you read?" or "When was the last time you heard something that surprised you?" Etter-Smith can get a glimpse of how the applicants operate and whether they strive for growth and development.

"If people can't answer those questions, they're just doing the same thing," she says. "It's like making the same doggone doughnuts every day." Those are the people who show up just to collect a paycheck. They lack the motivation and willingness to do more than the bare minimum. Leaders need to be able to pick out the low performers during the hiring process before they become a full-time problem.

Women's Leadership Challenges

The bar is higher for women in the workplace. While this may be a heated topic, it can't be ignored that there is unconscious bias that places women and minorities at a disadvantage.

"Whether it's explicit or implied, women leaders are almost always expected to behave like men," says Etter-Smith. "We're supposed to communicate in a way that's similar to men—very precise. We're not supposed to have any emotional attachment."

Over the course of her career, Etter-Smith has been accused of being too emotional on more than a few occasions. "I have never, in my twenty-five years of doing this, ever heard a man say to another man, 'Let's take emotions out of it.' Never."

When women become too passionate about a situation, it's often viewed as a negative. When men show emotion, it's viewed as strong leadership. It's not just emotions that women need to be conscious of in order to be taken seriously in the workplace. From their business attire to their tone of voice, women must navigate around seemingly trivial things that men never have to consider in their day-to-day lives. That's where bias emerges.

Men need to be more conscious about these "trivial things" to move the bar for women. They also need to realize that women value their work just as much as men.

"I think it's really time for men to step up," believes Etter-Smith. Across all industries, the boardroom is still heavily dominated by men. "The idea that women are responsible in some way for that—for making that change is a fallacy," she says. "The only way that changes is if men make that change."

Men must advocate on behalf of women in leadership. They must realize that they can make a positive, lasting impact for future women—which includes their daughters and granddaughters. They can't be blind enough to think that what is happening now doesn't impact their daughter's future. They must set them up for success.

Fluid Leadership

"Over the course of decades, people have remained the same. They're the one constant. It's the circumstances, the technology, and the jobs that change—and people adapt to those changes," says Etter-Smith. All these changes fuel different approaches to leadership.

We've moved beyond a nation of assembly lines into a more autonomous workforce. With the evolution of independent work and more people working outside of the office, the future of leadership will likely be more fluid, with people leading themselves, believes Etter-Smith.

The market may be changing rapidly, but great leadership is needed to navigate through these changes. Etter-Smith believes that leaders must remember that employees are actually volunteers. They don't invest their time or effort simply because of the paycheck. While the money is a perk, it's not the ultimate driver of employee engagement. Leaders need to be mindful that employees have the option to invest their time and energy into their projects. It's not a given. For that reason, leaders need to earn the trust of their employees and turn those volunteer hours into a productive outcome.

LEADERSHIP LESSON

"Expectations for women leaders are higher than they are for men." Agree or disagree? Explain your rationale.

Who was/is your leadership mentor?

What did your mentor do that encouraged or enhanced your leadership development?

What actions can you take to intentionally encourage or enhance the leadership development of someone in your organization?

DAVID BRENNAN

Author Introduction

In talking with David Brennan about leadership, you are quickly reminded how thoughtful and reflective great leaders truly are. You are also reminded that no leader, regardless of the success they have achieved or the accolades they have received, attained that status without a regret or two. When asked to reflect on his development as a leader, Brennan candidly recounts an event that took place almost forty years ago. It is, quite obviously, a painful memory, and he recalls it with such vivid accuracy you would swear he was speaking about something that happened yesterday.

He was six months into his first job in management. As a district manager, he was responsible for the commercial performance of 10-12 territory representatives, a job he had performed with distinction prior to his promotion. When he was in that role, he was driven by a sense of achievement, task focus, and performance success that separated him from his peers. Many in that capacity sought to master the features and benefits of their products and effectively articulate them to targeted customers. By comparison, Brennan was the kind of territory representative that sought to be able to detail competitive products better than his competitors before discussing his own. That took work. That took drive. That took a level of commitment and dedication that was comparatively unique.

As a manager, he became frustrated in the absence of similar drive on the part of his direct reports. One of his representatives personified this irritation. He had been a territory representative his entire career, over twenty years. He did his job. He hit his numbers. He moved on. Brennan took it upon himself to instill a heightened sense of purpose in this tenured employee. That effort culminated with this representative prematurely retiring. When Brennan asked him why, he received the following explanation, "I don't ever want to have to work for an asshole like you again."

The circumstances that surrounded that exchange had a profound impact on a young manager who would eventually become the CEO of one of the world's largest pharmaceutical companies. Management, in a very real sense, became something that was focused on tasks and milestones and articulated goals. Those goals are either hit, missed, or exceeded. The more significant the goal, the more uncomfortable it will be for the people responsible for producing it. Some grasp that reality as they embark on the journey. Others, perhaps most, have no idea what they are really getting into until they come face-to-face with a degree of adversity that can be immobilizing. Good managers help people navigate the periodic uncertainty that accompanies the accomplishment of targeted achievement.

By comparison, leadership is about objective intuition. It is a process that has far more to do with the unique needs of the people you are attempting to influence than it does with your predefined level of comfort in the face of an emergent challenge. As Brennan learned early, developing objective intuition takes some time. It's about creating a relationship with a spectrum of colleagues around the work that needs to be accomplished and occasionally asking questions like, "Is there something impeding your performance that has nothing to do with your skill level?"

As his career progressed, Brennan became acutely aware of the way many managers absolve their people of accountability with the absolute best of misguided intentions. Simply stated, when you are the boss and one of your direct reports approaches you, reveals they are struggling, and asks for your advice, red flags had better appear on your horizon! Because the minute you respond by telling them what you would do, you have dictated a course of action. In general terms, bosses cannot provide suggestions. Suggestions from bosses are orders, even when they are fully intended to be suggestions. As a matter of personal experience, Brennan suggests the higher you go in an organization you not only have to monitor the advice you give but the questions you ask. Because when you are the CEO and you ask for the time, subgroups may well be formed to try and determine, "What do you think he means by ... time?"

Above all else, the thing you garner from spending time with Brennan is the importance of taking complicated things and making them simple. When people are clear on what needs to be done, they can act. When they act, they can achieve results. It is preferable (of course) when everyone taking action understands and embraces the over-arching strategy, but the most important thing is that they are clear on what they are doing and how they should do it. In his words:

> "It's like walking past a construction site and asking a brick layer what he's doing. The first guy might look at you like you are a nuisance and say, 'I'm putting mortar on this brick.' A second might take a step back and tell you, 'We're building a wall.' A third might pause, look you in the eye and say, 'We're constructing a cathedral!' As a leader, all three can be instrumental in getting you where you need to go."

"Leadership is a delicate balance of people and task."

– David Brennan

PAY CLOSER ATTENTION
David Brennan

Management and Leadership

"Leadership is a delicate balance of people and task." It's more than achieving goals and turning losses into profits; leadership is about mentoring, coaching, and inspiring the people who are working toward your goals. Great leaders connect with their employees on a personal level.

David Brennan, former chief executive officer and executive director of AstraZeneca PLC, has spent his career refining his leadership approach. As a task-oriented person, Brennan found it much easier to focus on the task at hand than the personal side of business. It took time for him to learn how to balance people and purpose.

"I've always been of the persuasion that it's easier to train management skill than it is to train leadership," says Brennan. Leadership is not a skill that can be learned in a single training course; it's much more of a journey that requires development over time. That journey is different for every leader and requires different areas of focus.

Stepping into Management

Brennan began his career as a pharmaceutical sales representative at Merck. Through a combination of ambition and a love for sales, Brennan developed an ethical and straightforward sales approach that proved successful. Brennan set himself apart from his colleagues through his extensive research on competitive products, which allowed him to engage in higher-level conversations with physicians.

Brennan didn't use this approach to gain accolades and attention. He knew this was how he was going to be effective in a hospital environment where the residents were highly educated and valued learning. "You've got to be able to engage them at their level," says Brennan. By studying the competition and the market, Brennan yielded high sales and was rewarded with a promotion to management.

Brennan carried this goal-based mindset into his first management position—but did not achieve the same outcome. "I was probably a bit abrasive as a manager at times because I was so focused on an endpoint," says Brennan, "and if somebody couldn't get there at the speed with which I thought we should get there, they would be taken aback a little bit."

In fact, it took candid feedback from his employees for Brennan to gain perspective on the impact of his behavior. "I didn't realize it," says Brennan. "It made me step back and say, 'I need to be much more self-aware. I need to be much more empathetic. I need to be self-deprecating to some degree to be able to connect differently with different kinds of people.'"

While some employees may respond to a direct, no fluff management style, most employees want managers who are approachable and authentic. They want to know the person behind the suit and relate to them on a personal level. While this may require vulnerability on the part of the leader, the outcome is a more engaged and productive team.

A person's leadership style is cultivated based on his personality and the culture of the organization. While Brennan preferred to focus on goals and objectives, the culture at Merck reinforced this behavior with a performance-based philosophy. This approach was standard during this era of business, where the focus was largely on profits versus people. As the business world began to change, so did company culture and leadership approaches.

Leadership Lessons

A leader is shaped by his experiences—both good and bad. Despite taking advantage of fundamental management training courses offered by Merck, Brennan still had a lot to learn in terms of leadership. Over the course of his career, Brennan recalls two defining leadership lessons.

The first lesson involved the first person he ever hired. Brennan invested countless hours into training this sales rep in order to get him to the right level. Ultimately, he was not the right fit for the job, but Brennan persisted. "It was the age-old, self-fulfilling prophecy, 'I hired him, so I'm going to make him good,'" says Brennan.

It took one of Brennan's executive professional representatives, a twenty-five-year veteran in the field, who sat him down at lunch one day and said, "A few of us have been talking and you're not spending enough time with us because you're spending all that time with this guy, and he's probably not going to make it. You're really missing an opportunity to go to your strengths rather than focusing on your weakness, and you've got to help us with that, because you're good when you're out in the field with us."

This conversation made Brennan reevaluate how he spent his time and how willing he was to step up to a mistake he made in hiring. Upon reflection, Brennan met with his region manager to let him know that the sales rep wasn't going to work out and they needed to let him go. His boss replied, "Oh, I knew that a couple months ago. I was waiting for you to get there and I'm glad you did!"

Brennan was caught off guard with this admission, wondering why he didn't say something sooner. But he later realized that the job of the region manager is to make sure the district managers (DM) learn their job well, and hiring the right people is one of those things that a DM must learn.

The next valuable leadership lesson involved a sales representative with twenty years of experience who never exhibited high performance. This man did the bare minimum, achieving average performance ratings, and was content staying at the same level throughout his career. Hoping to increase his performance, Brennan began pushing this sales rep. Using his task-oriented mindset, Brennan took a more aggressive approach rather than coaching the sales rep on his areas of weakness.

One Saturday afternoon, after an exhausting business trip, Brennan received a phone call from this sales rep. He wanted to resign from the company. Brennan pressed him to understand why he was resigning after twenty years of service with the company. He said, "I just want you to know I'm resigning. So now you know." And he hung up.

Brennan called his region manager to tell him about the resignation. His boss was adamant that they couldn't just let a twenty-year sales professional resign. Brennan agreed and explained that he tried to tell him that but he wouldn't listen. His boss proposed that they make a visit to the sales rep's home. They drove to his apartment, parked the car, and walked up the back steps.

What unfolded next is still pressed into Brennan's memory as one of his most valuable leadership lessons. The living room was empty, with the sales rep sitting in a lounge chair surrounded by pictures of his daughters and wife, and a gun sitting next to him. He was, perhaps, moments away from committing suicide.

Luckily, Brennan and his boss were able to talk with the sales rep and took him to a treatment center, where he stayed for a month or two. Brennan intended to hold his sales territory open while he was seeking treatment, but the man said, "I don't ever want to have to work for an asshole like you again, so I'm going to retire."

This was the first time that Brennan learned the circumstances of this man's life. His wife recently passed away and his daughters thought he stole the insurance money. They disowned him and he was abandoned by his family. This man's whole world collapsed and Brennan had no idea. Brennan never asked him one question about his personal life. He asked him plenty of questions about product information, routing, and territories but never one about his personal life.

This situation opened Brennan's eyes to the importance of understanding the circumstances of your employees' lives. "Leaders must pay closer attention—not just to the work but to the person," says Brennan. Talk to your employees to understand if there are circumstances preventing them from reaching their goals. It's often easier to keep the conversation on business, but sometimes it can be a matter of life or death, as in Brennan's case.

Understanding the Why

Employees are more motivated and productive when they understand the purpose behind a goal or objective. They need to connect with the goal and understand how their performance makes a difference. Brennan first learned this message as a college football player.

Brennan, a sophomore, made the starting offensive line and beat out a close friend of his, Bill Hind, a senior offensive guard. Brennan feared there would be a bit of resentment over the matter, but he soon came to realize that Hind's focus was on the success of the offensive line. Regardless of his feelings toward Brennan, Hind understood that the coach had his reasons for the team's lineup and his focus was on the team, not himself. He was able to separate his emotions from the end goal—winning a football game.

Brennan was met with this challenge throughout his business career. "I found in my work experience, you're challenged at times to step into a situation where not everybody is going to be comfortable with the perspective you bring or the decision you are going to make that's going to affect the group," he says. "When you have the 'why' clear in your mind about what you are going to do, it's easier to step up, even if it makes people uncomfortable."

People need to believe in what they're doing. They want to contribute toward something important and impactful. This motivation to seek meaningful work is what drives employees and leaders need to help employees make those connections.

Building Trust and Accountability

Effective leadership is about fostering collaboration, building trust, and breaking down barriers in the workplace. Leaders must work to deemphasize their position power and connect with their employees.

"You have to get people to see you and to know you as a person so they recognize that you're no different from them," says Brennan. "You may have a different position than they have, but you're a human being and that person's a human being, and we need to be able to connect at that level."

At the most fundamental level, leaders must have a relationship with their employees. It doesn't necessarily have to be personal, but it does need to be at a level that establishes trust and accountability.

When Brennan assumed the role of CEO at AstraZeneca, he was surprised at how much the rest of the management team asked for his advice. There was a sincere absence of true accountability due to the structure the previous CEO had in place. He would essentially tell the executive team what to do when he was approached with questions. While the previous CEO was comfortable in that role, Brennan was not. Brennan couldn't wrap his head around why an operations guy would ask for his advice when Brennan was not the operations expert.

Brennan set out to change the dynamics of delegation by alleviating the need for managers to ask for budget approvals so frequently. He received some backlash from board members questioning this shift. "I was trying to push accountability down into the organization and one of the markers for that, one of the things that people follow, is the grant of authority," says Brennan.

Brennan set into motion a new accountability structure which changed his contract with employees. He instilled confidence in his team to make decisions and own them. Brennan viewed the c-suite as a team of experts. For the organization to run more smoothly, everyone needed to own their piece—and that starts with trust.

Straight Shooter

Brennan's straightforward approach to life and business has allowed him to achieve great success. He has increased company earnings, brought accountability to the forefront of organizations, and impacted change on many levels. His leadership journey has enabled him to better connect with others and foster relationships with those that he serves. At the end of the day, profits are important to achieve, but as Brennan has learned, it's the people who are, ultimately, core to the business.

LEADERSHIP LESSON

Consider the statements below and self-assess based on the following scale: 1—Highly ineffective; 3—OK; 5—Highly effective.

How are you at forming a relationship with others around the work to be done?

Identify one specific action you can take to improve.

How are you at ensuring members of your team understand the purpose behind the work they are doing?

Identify one specific action you can take to ensure that understanding.

Providing direct reports with advice or suggestions on how to solve problems makes holding them accountable for results more difficult. Agree or disagree? Explain your rationale.

SHEILA SIMON

Author Introduction

For some strange reason, when you do a little digging into Sheila Simon's background, a classic scene from the movie *My Cousin Vinny* comes to mind. It's the courtroom scene toward the end of the film where Vinny Gambini (Joe Pesci) calls his girlfriend, Mona Lisa Vito (Marisa Tomei), to testify as an expert automotive witness in a murder trial. The prosecutor is skeptical and asks Ms. Vito to explain the nature of her qualifications. Ms. Vito explains:

- her father was a mechanic.

- her uncles were mechanics.

- her brothers are mechanics.

And, as such, she grew up in a repair shop performing any number of engine-related procedures herself, because that's what her family did! When the prosecutor is finally convinced her experience meets the necessary requirements, she is permitted to testify and justice winds up being served in a highly entertaining manner!

Along similar lines there is very little doubt that Simon's upbringing qualifies her as an expert in the realm of

American politics. Her mother, Jeanne Hurley Simon, and father, Paul Simon, were members of the Illinois House of Representatives. Paul Simon went on to serve as the lieutenant governor of Illinois, a member of the United States House of Representatives (1975-85), the United States Senate (1985-97), and ran for president in 1988. In a very real, hands-on manner, Simon grew up immersed in American politics very much aware of what leaders did and how they went about doing it!

Given those givens it should surprise absolutely no one that Simon followed in her parents' footsteps after graduating from law school at Georgetown. She was a member of llinois' Carbondale City Council, an assistant state's attorney, and the forty-sixth lieutenant governor of Illinois. Her political career has known both victory and defeat. She could best be described as a person who won with inspirational grace and lost with unifying dignity. In that regard, it should come as no surprise that Simon views any experience—win or lose—as an opportunity to learn something important!

When she first became lieutenant governor, Simon was immediately tasked with the responsibility to hire her staff. After what seemed like careful deliberation, she made her choices. With the best of intentions, a member of her inner circle pointed out that there were a significant number of women on the team, and there could well be unintended political consequences as a result.

Simon considered the observation, examined the gender makeup of her colleagues' staff, mostly men, and concluded that since her staff had, indeed, been chosen on merit, that was the last thing she needed to be worrying about!

When she isn't holding office, she is an associate law professor at Southern Illinois University and is frequently described as "uber smart." When she enters a room, her brain comes in first and everything else just sort of follows! Right alongside all of that, she is patient, and caring, and literally infused with humility. Not the self-deprecating kind, but the kind that recognizes the importance of every person and every perspective, whether she happens to agree with it or not.

Simon recognizes the great strides that women in leadership have made during the twentieth and twenty-first centuries. She also recognizes that there is much more work to be done for the nuances of female leadership—whether in politics or business—to become fully appreciated.

"Leaders help people learn."

- Sheila Simon

JUST KEEP PUSHING

Sheila Simon

Passion for the Positive

A civil servant is driven by a passion and interest in helping others and making a positive impact on their community. Sheila Simon, former lieutenant governor of Illinois, has dedicated her professional life to serving and educating others.

From being an attorney and associate law professor to serving as a city council member and a lieutenant governor, Simon enjoys engaging with the public to influence change. While Simon now boasts an impressive resume of leadership positions, her political career emerged with limited fanfare given her heritage.

Passion and Politics

As the daughter of former U.S. Senator Paul Simon and former Illinois State Representative Jeanne Hurley Simon, Sheila Simon learned about leadership from her parents. In particular, she recalls asking her mother how she decided to vote on matters. Her mother explained that connecting with like-minded and trustworthy people who share similar values was one of her best resources for making tough decisions. In fact, that alignment around key issues led her mother to meet her father.

Growing up with this leadership influence, Simon naturally gravitated toward leadership roles throughout her life. As president of the student government at Wittenberg University in Springfield, Ohio, Simon led a charge to require foreign language study. Up to that point, it had been optional, but the students thought it would add to the value of their degrees if every Wittenberg graduate had a foreign language background.

Simon went on to assume more serious leadership roles on the Carbondale City Council—which was not a position she intentionally targeted. It was a neighbor who informed her that the city was expanding the size of its city council and encouraged her to get involved. This intrigued Simon so she decided to run for city council.

Serving as a council member for four years, Simon focused her efforts on getting more people engaged in local government and informing the public of their service projects. During this time, Simon was not fond of the way the mayor was running the city and took a big leap and decided to run. While the election resulted in a loss for Simon, she was not discouraged—she relished in the impact of her campaign and found enjoyment in the effort she and her team put forth.

In 2010, Simon's political career took an unexpected turn when she became the lieutenant governor of Illinois. During the Democratic primary, Scott Lee Cohen secured the win. Just five days after the election, he withdrew amid controversy in his personal life that was brought to light from the media. This left the Democratic party scrambling to replace him on the election ballot. Acknowledging that everyone on the statewide ticket was from Cook County, the county where Chicago is located, the party members thought it would be advantageous to pick someone from southern Illinois.

Simon, located in southern Illinois, emerged as a possible contender through her work with the city council. The selection process required her to give speeches before the panel of party leaders and at the statewide meeting. She was eventually selected by the party as Illinois Governor Pat Quinn's running mate in the general election. The duo secured the win and Simon went on to serve as lieutenant governor for the next four years.

Lessons Learned

A leader is not necessarily the loudest person in the room or the most senior member of staff. A leader identifies herself as the person who imparts knowledge or encourages others who may need help. "Leaders help people learn," says Simon, "they nudge rather than drag people to places they otherwise would not have gone."

Simon learned the importance of taking the time to share knowledge from her close friend Dawn Clark Netsch, the first woman elected as the comptroller of Illinois. Netsch was also in the running for governor against Governor Jim Edgar, which made her the first woman to receive a major-party nomination for governor.

During a press conference, Simon recalls a moment that still sticks with her. Netsch was discussing the state budget and was extremely knowledgeable about the entire process. "She took the time to answer every reporter's question down to the last detail," says Simon. "It was brilliant."

While Netsch lost the election, it left a huge impression on Simon. "It was really a model for me in terms of how you really need to know what you're doing and what you're talking about and take the time to explain it to other people so that they can get on board with you," she says. It's this level of buy-in that is critical to successful leadership.

Leadership Challenges for Women
While women have made great strides in leadership, there's still an obvious gender gap when looking at the number of women occupying senior positions. There are many reasons contributing to this gap, but Simon believes that there are noticeable distinctions in how men and women approach leadership.

"It's not that women are lacking confidence, it's that sometimes men have unearned overconfidence," she says. Men are more likely to think, "I know I'm right," and quickly move forward with implementing his idea or solution. A woman is oftentimes more thoughtful with gathering input from a variety of people before formulating a solution. In general, there's more collaboration and less assumption on the part of women. While this isn't indicative to everyone, women are more likely to achieve a solution through teamwork.

"Recognizing that we need to have different points of view is really important," says Simon. When serving as the lieutenant governor, she hired many qualified women to fill senior roles on her team. Upon reflection, Simon believes there is still a lot of work to be done in terms of gender equality in leadership. Until all the boardrooms across the country are diverse, progress still needs to be made.

Pushing the Issues

Leadership isn't all about compliments or acknowledgement. It's about passion, drive, and dedication to serving others. Simon learned the importance of persistence to drive results during her term as lieutenant governor.

One of the projects that Simon actively pursued in office was trying to get a better disclosure law for elected officials in the state of Illinois. The state had an outdated form that collected minimal information from elected officials. In fact, you could answer "not applicable" or "none" to most of the questions even if you were answering everything in a very straightforward way. Reporters called it the "none sheet" because so many people just answered "none" to everything.

Updating the form made many legislators uncomfortable with the idea of having to disclose all their financial earnings. Simon and her team pushed the issue so citizens could have full transparency when casting their vote to ensure legislators didn't have any underlying conflicts of interest.

The legislation was eventually passed in the Senate but got held up in the House of Representatives. The House leadership assured Simon that they were working on it and the legislation was in committee. However, the legislation did not get passed, which frustrated and stunned Simon. In retrospect, Simon believes leadership simply brushed their idea to the side but, at the time, she believed they were really working on it.

"I think my failure on that was not really pushing it harder," says Simon. "I learned to keep pushing." And this lesson is indicative to the success of any leader. To be successful, a leader must stay focused on the desired goal and keep pushing until they achieve results.

LEADERSHIP LESSON

Leaders "nudge" rather than "drag." Agree or disagree? Explain your rationale.

Based on your experience, what is the source of a leader's confidence?

Identify three things you can do to help others develop the confidence necessary to effectively lead others.

PAT SUMMITT

Author Introduction

There are people in life that, somewhere along the way, become consumed by what they don't have. They aren't tall enough, or smart enough, or rich enough, or attractive enough, etc. With those folks, sooner or later the phrase "if only …" works its way into their conversations.

On the other hand, thankfully, there are people like Pat Summitt. It would not be exaggerating to suggest that Summitt lived every minute of her life appreciating what she had while simultaneously trying her very best to make the most of it. When you asked her about that, she would quickly explain that she came by those traits honestly. She grew up on a farm in rural Tennessee with a father that not only modeled that life philosophy, he made it his personal mission to communicate the value of that approach to those around him.

When you dug a little deeper to find out what that was like, she would immediately smile a reflective smile while a tear or two literally formed in her eyes and say, "It wasn't easy." And it probably wasn't. Like most any other kid growing up anywhere in the world, young Summitt gravitated toward "fun." She would wonder why she had to get up so early and come home immediately after school to do chores around the farm while her peers had no such requirements. But she complied and somewhere along the way, it clicked! She discovered there was inherent, inescapable self-satisfaction and virtue that could be derived from reliably fulfilling your obligations to the absolute best of your ability. Beyond that, the journey was, indeed, the reward! It simply "felt right" to get the most out of whatever potential you had been blessed with each time you had the opportunity to put that potential in motion.

As most, if not all, of us are aware by now, the achievement orientation she learned on the farm was put on active display for decades as a Hall of Fame basketball coach at The University of Tennessee. An All-American player in college and an Olympic co-captain on a silver-medal team in the 1976 Summer Games, Summitt became the head coach of the University of Tennessee Volunteers at the ripe old age of twenty-two. She would go on to coach the Lady Volunteers for thirty-eight years to 1,098 victories (an average of twenty-eight per year!). Among many other accolades during her career, she was named NCAA Coach of the Year seven times, won eight NCCA Championships, an Olympic gold medal, received the Presidential Medal of Freedom, and won The Arthur Ashe Courage Award.

Despite all of that, the one thing that stood out about Summitt when you had the honor to be in her presence was her humility. She would routinely explain away one accomplishment after another as being a function of "being in the right place at the right time." When you would point out that it certainly seemed as though she had been "at the right place at the right time" quite a bit during her career, she would fire right back with a homespun line like this:

"You know ... all I can say is when you see a turtle sitting on a fence post ... you know he didn't get there by himself!"[1]

Like many leaders that truly leave their mark on the world, Summitt's impact far transcended the realm of women's athletics. In Summitt's case, her mark was defined by the terms "simplicity" and "execution." You want to be successful in life? Quit worrying about what you don't have! Get up early! Apply yourself! Get the most you can possibly get out of the talent you have been given! Is that easy? Heck no! Is it worth it? Yes.

Evidently that message still resonates. Forty-five former players that gave their all for Summitt are coaching today, which is comforting news. Because even though Summitt left us far too early (in 2016), her legacy might live on forever!

---

[1]Shriver, Sam. *From Coach to Coach: Real World Wisdom from the Athletic Industry's Finest.* Fulcourt Press, 1989. Shriver interviewed Coach Summitt at the University of Tennessee during the 1987-88 basketball season. Unless otherwise cited, Coach Summitt's quotes are excerpts from this book.

"I would not ask my staff or my team to do anything that I wouldn't do myself."

- Pat Summitt

WINNING IS NOT THE POINT!

Pat Summitt

The Steely-Eyed Stare

How do we remember "the greats" in any field?

Is it because of what they accomplished? The way they touched the lives of those they encountered? The words they said?

All of those things matter, for sure. But when we scratch beneath the surface, we find that truly powerful leadership is by example. No one exemplified this better than legendary Tennessee women's basketball coach, Pat Summitt.

The person we remember today as the disciplinarian with the blue, steely-eyed stare and stoic expression was one of the greatest competitors to ever grace the American sporting landscape.

Much more than that, Summitt was a winner—both on and off the court. She was the first Division 1 basketball coach to reach 1,000 wins. She won a staggering eight national championships. Yet, to know her story for only the championships and wins would be missing the point.

Summitt's life was a quest to positively impact the lives of as many people as she could. She demanded a tremendous amount from her administration, coaches, staff, and players. She demanded more from herself. This drive to be the best—and to show others how to be their best—is central to the leadership message she gifted to all of us.

Raised on the Farm
Summitt (né Head) graduated in 1974 from the University of Tennessee at Martin (UT Martin), but the best education she ever received came on the Head family dairy and tobacco farm in Clarksville, Tennessee.

During this time on the farm, Summitt learned what hard work, discipline, dedication, and commitment were all about. Her family's livelihood depended on it. Her father, Richard Head, was a strict disciplinarian who instilled both fear and very valuable life lessons in his children. He was a powerful authority figure that taught his daughter to refuse to accept anything less than the best standard for how to do everything.

Chores were plentiful on the Head farm, and yet there was also time for basketball after the day's work was finished. It was there that she learned the game that would become the tool for how she brought leadership and life lessons—not just to her players—but to millions of people.

The Drive for More
In her early teen years, the family moved just over the county line to Henrietta, Tennessee so that young Summitt could play high school basketball. At a time where women

were still fighting to gain acceptance in high school and college sports, this was a tremendously altruistic gesture by her father who saw so much potential in his daughter.

Summitt blossomed and, after a stellar high school career, later went on to play basketball at UT Martin. Following graduation, she pursued a master's degree at the University of Tennessee (UT). She joined the basketball program and then unexpectedly found herself in the head coach's seat when the previous coach abruptly quit. Just like that, at age twenty-two, Summit was the head women's basketball coach at the University of Tennessee.

She even drove the team bus in those early years. Her salary? Two hundred fifty dollars a month, a far cry from today's multimillion-dollar coaching salaries. To say Summitt was doing it "for the love of the game" would be an understatement.

She later earned a place on the 1976 U.S. Olympic women's basketball team and co-captained the team to a silver medal at the Montreal summer games, an incredible feat given her other professional responsibilities.

A Standard of Excellence

Summit had a way of running the UT basketball program that left an unmistakable impression on anyone that came across the Lady Vols: "We're going to prepare more than you. We're going to outwork you. We're going to focus on every fundamental of the game and ensure we are the best in every area. And that's just Tuesday. Because we're coming back again tomorrow, and again ..."

Summitt's consistency of approach came from a servant leader's heart. She genuinely led with empathy, which was the true secret to her success. The truth is, both sports and business history are littered with "leaders" that demanded infinite amounts from their players and employees. What separated Summitt from other leaders wasn't just the way she ran the UT women's basketball operation. It was the way she treated people.

In the truly intense moments of competition, players knew no one had their backs more than Summitt. Everyone around her knew that she would never ask them to do anything that she hadn't done—or wouldn't do—herself. It was this commitment to excellence that ingratiated her to the women who played for her and the fans that bleed orange and white.

Furthermore, it was her level of devotion and care for making her players the most well-rounded women they could be. Every player who completed her eligibility under Summitt—in thirty-eight years—graduated with a degree from the University of Tennessee. Even in her later years, she would still check in with faculty at UT to make sure her players were attending class. No stone left unturned. No detail missed. Summitt knew that a truly great leader always covered every angle.

The Leader Behind the Stare

What made Summitt so special was her genuine interest in helping everyone in her life. She always asked how everyone was doing. As gracious as she was hospitable, she showed people that she cared and astutely understood how important this was to leading and a winning foundation.

She was very concerned and grounded in the "what" and the "how." This amounted to painstaking preparation that started the moment she made contact with a potential recruit. From selling herself, to the UT program, to demonstrating what, how, and why they were the best program in the country, Summitt had preparation covered. Her message: No one is going to get the job done more effectively than us. And that begins with my leadership.

Summitt saw herself as the perennial overachiever. It's how she viewed herself at a young age and how she saw her older brother, who played college basketball at Austin Peay State University. She described herself as someone that didn't have all the talent but was motivated each day and had a great work ethic. She mastered two things we can always control—our attitude and our effort.

Summitt believed self-confidence could be taught. She made this her mission as head coach. Countless high school All-Americans entered through the halls of Thompson-Boling arena in Knoxville, and yet these highly talented young women discovered quickly that the mental and emotional side of the game would be more important than the physical. This is where Summitt thrived. She showed her players how to be mentally tough. She put them through the most rigorous practices and exercises of any program in the country.

Summitt had extremely high expectations of her players—but always of herself first. This leadership by example permeated the UT locker room and provided a much-needed boost of self-confidence to her players.

"Right off, we start with a high level of expectation. Like expecting an A in the classroom."

Prior to winning the 1987 national championship game, Summitt's Lady Vols had been to three Final Fours in the previous five seasons. So close, and yet so far. Before the resounding victory over Louisiana Tech that would give her the first of eight national championships, Summitt didn't resort to a rigorous, physical practice with yelling and pep talks.

Rather, she took the team through a silent visualization exercise. They sat around midcourt on the championship hardwood and imagined themselves playing great defense. They visualized making the big plays in the game that would give them a 67-44 victory. It paid off, big time. Tennessee's defensive effort was one for the ages. This boost in self-confidence was paramount in their preparation and game performance.

Family First

Every great leadership lesson that emanated from Summitt came from her love of family—her birth, married, and basketball families. Summitt used the term "family" when it came to leadership because to her that's what the Lady Vols were. They won and lost as a team and always stuck together and supported each other from the highest of highs to the lowest of lows. One thing very important to remember about every great champion is this: Anyone that's ever won at the highest level has endured crushing losses. Summitt knew from her earlier years and even as she progressed—keep in mind she lost in five national title games—that this discipline and close-knit family environment would sustain them through good times and bad.

Whenever she and her Lady Vols faced adversity, she was taken back to her dad on a tractor at the farm and the right way to do things. The chores that she learned on the farm were so valuable in molding her as a person. That is the genius of Summitt's leadership. Everything came back to those lessons on that farm in rural Tennessee. Commitment, discipline, hard work, respect, and care for one another. She took this into the very complicated world of Division 1 sports that is often rife with temptations and opportunities to take shortcuts and created a winning program that handled its business the right way. "The best leadership approach to get the end results that you want is to get people to work together. We'd have twenty-four hours prior to a game to think about that game. Twenty-four hours after a game to think about what happened—whether we won or lost. But not to dwell on it. That's a form of discipline that we established together."

Summitt's life was one of high expectations, for herself and the people under her. She was a conduit through which other people discovered their maximum potential in life. She began each season with individualized goal setting for her players. Midway through the season, she'd revisit those goals, all while keeping her own score as the year played out. At season's end it was time for evaluation and reflection. What went well? What didn't? Always—how do we get better?

She fervently believed in letting each talented player exercise her strengths to the greatest degree as long as it was within the team concept.

Great leaders always need to have a plan. It's wise to gather feedback, concepts, and strategies from others but ultimately, you need your own plan for what is going to work for you and your team. Discipline was paramount for her. She recognized she needed to set this discipline and tone by example. Having the direction of where and then how to get there. She'd be the guide. That was the Tennessee way.

A Competitor to the End

"No one feels strong when she examines her own weakness. But in facing weakness, you learn how much there is in you, and you find real strength,"[2] said Summitt. In August of 2011, just before the start of her final season with the Lady Vols, Summitt announced that she had early onset dementia in the form of Alzheimer's—a terrible disease that would unfortunately claim her life less than five years later.

As fierce a competitor as she was on the court, Summitt was as valiant and courageous in her public and private handling of the disease. She lived each day with a championship mindset, never wanting anyone to feel sorry for her. All the way to the end, Summit was a leader who provided an example to everyone on how to live a fulfilling, brave life.

---

[2]The Pat Summitt Foundation. Pat Summitt Motivational Monday Quote. *Facebook*, 27 Apr. 2020, 9:59 a.m. https://m.facebook.com/PatSummittFoundation/posts/3247678341938460. Accessed 3 Nov. 2020.

On the Mount Rushmore of sports coaches, Summitt deserves her rightful place. As we all know, nothing great ever comes easy. Nothing worth doing gets handed to us. We have to work for it. As she was fond of saying, "Getting to the top comes from a commitment from within."

When the photographers, TV cameras, and confetti go away, we find ourselves looking back into that mirror of life. What will that reflection show us? That we were proud of what we did? Will it really be about the trophies or accolades? While Summitt had those, for her it was truly about the lives she touched. The ladies that she developed into proud, confident, intelligent, strong women. That was what it was all about.

The Rewards Are Worth the Cost

"To me, teamwork is a lot like being part of a family. It comes with obligations, entanglements, headaches, and quarrels. But the rewards are worth the cost,"[3] said Summit. As Tom Hanks' Jimmy Dugan famously says to Geena Davis' character, Dottie, in *A League of Their Own*, "It's supposed to be hard. If it wasn't hard, everyone would do it. The hard is what makes it great." In Summitt's own inimitable way, she proved that true personal and professional growth never comes easy. From the days of working from sunup, to sundown on that farm in Clarksville, Summitt developed into a great leader because she wanted it so badly—because she was willing to put in the hard work.

---

[3]Roberts, Daron K. "Leadership Lessons from Legendary Basketball Coach Pat Summitt." *Forbes Magazine*, 5 July 2016, 6:36 p.m. www.forbes.com/sites/daronroberts/2016/07/02/leadership-lessons-from-legendary-basketball-coach-pat-summitt. Accessed 3 Nov. 2020.

In leadership, like in life, it's rare that we find people who truly live by action every great word they speak. Values, morals, and principles are fine and dandy, but when they're not backed up by actions, they become just another speech. Summitt knew in her mind and heart that she would give maximum effort and positive attitude to every day. Everyone around her knew it—and counted on it. This provided stability and consistency—key underpinnings of successful leadership.

She had no problem driving people to levels of performance that they never dreamed of. She expected as much out of them as she did herself. Those expectations got bigger and bolder each year. This incredible leadership power—that every one of us controls—became infectious and, ultimately, led to her scaling the mountaintop of her sport in a way no one ever has.

In leadership, people tend to adopt an approach that is more nurturing and collaborative, and they remove personal accountability from the equation. That was never Summitt. She once said, "If you're not up for the type of challenges that hold up to our level of standard, then maybe there's another place for you."

Summitt knew that in order to effectively reach people— to get them to maximize their abilities and potential—she needed to show that she genuinely cared. Her tough-love approach, beyond the bold exterior, was one of remarkable emotional intelligence and poise. Those that knew her closest remember her best by that approach.

It's best to close with her own words. These come from a letter she wrote to one of her former players prior to her starting her first game at Tennessee. Reflect on the words and you'll understand what it meant to be led by the great Coach Summitt:

> "... winning's nice. It's a good feeling. Like the whole world is yours. But it passes, this feeling. And what lasts is what you've learned. And what you've learned about is—life! ... Winning is fun ... Sure.

> But winning is not the point.
> Wanting to win is the point.
> Not giving up is the point.
> Never letting up is the point.
> Never being satisfied with what you've done is the point.

> The game is never over. No matter what the scoreboard reads, or what the referee says, it doesn't end when you come off the court.

> The secret of the game is in doing your best. To persist and endure, 'to strive, to seek, to find, and not to yield.'"[4]

---

[4]Jenkins, Sally. "'The Game Is Never Over:' A Letter from Pat Summitt to a Young Basketball Player." *The Washington Post*, 28 June 2016. http://www.washingtonpost.com/sports/colleges/widely-beloved-pat-summitt-was-cherished-most-by-those-who-saw-her-complexities/2016/06/28/581a391a-3d2e-11e6-80bc-d06711fd2125_story.html?noredirect=on. Accessed 3 Nov. 2020.

LEADERSHIP LESSON

What are your personal standards of excellence as a leader?

Self-confidence can be taught. Agree or disagree? Explain your rationale.

Winning is not the point. Agree or disagree? Explain your rationale.

CONCLUSION

Extraordinary leaders are committed to a lifetime of learning. As Sandy Ogg noted in the foreword, people learn the fundamental principles of leadership from other great leaders. And they master how to be a leader by applying those principles in diverse, real-world situations.

We hope that *Lessons from Leaders* will be a source of continual inspiration and guidance as you apply the practical lessons that have been shared in this book. This conclusion is the bridge to the lessons that have yet to be realized— the lessons that you will learn and experience on your own personal leadership journey. Because all the stories were so different and personal, you might be surprised to know that every leader interviewed for this book was asked the same nine questions. We have included those interview questions here and invite you to discover and cultivate your own personal leadership lessons.

Lessons from Leaders Interview Questions

1. How do you define leadership?

2. When did you first recognize or experience leadership?

3. Who are your personal leadership role models?

4. How have your role models influenced your leadership journey?

5. What role does leadership play in an organization's success?

6. How do you identify and develop leaders?

7. Think about your first management experience. What challenges did you come across and what lessons did you learn?

8. If you could share one leadership tip or piece of advice for managers, what would that be?

9. What do you want to be known for?

If you are interested in sharing your leadership lessons with us, reach out to us at share@lessonsfromleadersbook.com.

THE AUTHORS

Marshall Goldsmith is a Thinkers50 #1 executive coach and *New York Times* #1 best-selling author of *Triggers, Mojo,* and *What Got You Here Won't Get You There.*

Sam Shriver is the executive vice president of thought leadership and training transfer at The Center for Leadership Studies and the author of *From Coach to Coach* and *The Four Moments of Truth.* He received his BS from the United States Coast Guard Academy, MBA from Pepperdine University, and EdD from North Carolina State University.

Kathy McDermott is a managing partner at Global Coaching Alliance and the founder of McDermott & Associates Coaching, LLC. She has over twenty-five years of active experience as a corporate leader with Merck, Astra Merck, and AstraZeneca. Kathy graduated summa cum laude from Gwynedd Mercy University.

EVERYTHING A LEADER DOES MATTERS.

Anyone who has ever experienced the impact of poor leadership understands the significance of effective leadership. When a leader is doing the right things, we may not recognize every action or characteristic as "leadership" in the moment, but we can feel it. So how do we model that behavior?

The authors of *Lessons from Leaders* distill decades of experience from fifteen remarkable leaders into a collection of entertaining stories that will inspire and guide readers to transform the way they lead. Not based on one voice or perspective, this book features a diverse spectrum of leaders from all walks of life. Some are more recognizable than others, but their lessons are uniquely relatable and compelling.

The candid and illuminating accounts of each leader's vastly different personal leadership journey—the people and experiences that shaped their beliefs, practices, and priorities—reveal the essential skills and characteristics that define extraordinary leadership.

Lessons from Leaders is not steeped in theory or complexity but is grounded in personal truths that paint a consistent picture of who a leader is and what a leader does. Each chapter includes an actionable Leadership Lesson that outlines steps the reader can take to reflect and apply meaningful insights.

Not a book that will be read once and put on the shelf, leaders at every level will want to highlight enduring takeaways, make notes in the margins, and use *Lessons from Leaders* as a compass to guide their journey to becoming an extraordinary leader.